ROSES

ROSES

1001 Gardening Questions Answered

by
The Editors of Garden Way Publishing

Foreword by Peter Chan

A GARDEN WAY PUBLISHING BOOK

STOREY

STOREY COMMUNICATIONS, INC.
POWNAL, VERMONT 05261

Produced by Storey Communications, Inc.
President, M. John Storey
Executive Vice President of Administration, Martha M. Storey
Executive Vice President of Operations, Douglas B. Rhodes
Publisher, Thomas Woll

Written by Jack Kramer and the Editors of Garden Way Publishing
Cover and text design by Andrea Gray
Edited by Jeff Silva
Production by Andrea Gray and Rebecca Babbitt
Front cover photograph by Ann Reilly
Back cover photograph by Ann Reilly
Interior photographs by Andrew R. Addkison, Jack Barnich, Matthew
    Barr, Derek Fell, Jack Kramer, Maggie Oster, and Ann Reilly
Chapter opening photographs: Introduction, 1, 2, 3, and 4 by Ann
    Reilly; 5 by Derek Fell.
Drawings by Birgitta Fuhrmann, Adrián Martínez, Bob Johnson
Map by Northern Cartographic
Typesetting by The Best Type & Design on Earth, Burlington, VT

Library of Congress Catalog Card Number: 88-45619
International Standard Book Number: 0-88266-535-9 (hardcover)

Library of Congress Cataloging-in-Publication Data

Roses—: 1,001 gardening questions answered.

   Bibliography: p.
   Includes index.
   1. Rose culture—Miscellanea.   2. Roses—Miscellanea.
I. Garden Way Publishing,
SB411.R65992 1989   635.9′33372   88-45620
ISBN 0-88266-532-4

Contents

The rose, queen of flowers, is everyone's favorite, whether or not one is a gardener. Because it is suited to all kinds of landscaping needs, it is used in parks and home gardens throughout the world. For centuries roses have been seen as a symbol of romance, beauty, and elegance, and thus a bouquet of roses brings pleasure whether a gift from a dear friend, a lover, or a relative. The incomparable loveliness of the rose has no substitute.

Sylvia Chan

Rosaceae is a large family, including roses, apples, pears, and strawberries, among others. Species of *Rosa* can be found throughout the Northern Hemisphere, even in Alaska.

Roses are an ancient flower: fossilized wild roses have been discovered that date as far back as forty million years. Even prior to 2,500 B.C., the Chinese cultivated roses for the imperial garden, and from early times through the late eighteenth century, the Chinese tea trade with Europe included beautiful tea-scented, ever-blooming roses. In shades of red, crimson, pink, and yellow, these roses were prized in Empress Josephine's garden at Malmaison. So revered was this garden that when ships carrying those beautiful Chinese roses were captured during the Napoleonic Wars, gallant British sea captains sent the precious shrubs on to Malmaison.

The modern perpetual rose is the result of the French rose breeders' hard work. In 1867, La France, a successful hybrid descended from the Chinese tea rose and the standard European rose, was first marketed in France and soon became a favorite throughout the world. European and American rose breeders have since then created more than 20,000 varieties, among which 11,000 are hybrid tea roses, and new varieties are registered every year. Roses account for $1.5 billion worth of commerce in the United States every year, a figure that includes the sale of fifty million rose plants and more than 600 million cut flowers.

With their varying shapes, forms, colors, and especially their delightful perfume, roses surpass all other flowers in their length of bloom. Whereas other flowers bloom for a week to perhaps a month, all kinds of roses—hybrid teas, floribundas, grandifloras, and climbers—bloom from early summer on into fall. This characteristic alone in large measure explains their popularity.

Once you begin growing roses in your home garden, you will find that they are not as difficult as you may have been led to believe. It is true that you must be willing to spend a bit of time daily, or at least every other day, with your roses to keep them in top shape. You will feel so proud when your friends admire them, however, that the time spent will be well worth it. Although roses are hardy, you are more likely to succeed if you make an effort to acquire basic knowledge about the way to plant, fertilize, and prune roses, as well as how to control the diseases and insect pests that afflict them.

This book can be as handy to you as your watering can, for it answers the most common questions of rose growers everywhere. Use it as your reference and guide—and then go out and enjoy your roses!

Peter Chan
Master Gardener

ROSES

The Rose Through History

Roses have held an honored place in the hearts and gardens of mankind for more than 2,000 years. Even before roses were cultivated for their beauty, fragrance, and their purported medicinal value, they surely were appreciated in the wild: by studying fossil remains, scientists have determined that roses have been with us for forty million years more or less. Sappho, the Greek poet of the sixth century B.C., is credited with naming the rose the "Queen of Flowers":

> Would Jove appoint some flower to reign
> In matchless beauty on the plain,
> The Rose, mankind will all agree
> The Rose, the Queen of Flowers should be.

In the fourth century B.C., the Greek botanist Theophratus described various roses. The ancient city of Rhodes was named after the Greek word *rhodon*, which means *rose*. Assyrian and Babylonian architectural details featured the rose motif, but the Romans were the first to use roses as a garden plant. For weddings, funerals, or ceremonies and celebrations, thousands of roses were part of the activities. Indeed, the Romans' frenzied admiration of the flower made it into a symbol of extravagance and overindulgence.

When Rome fell, the rose fell, too, for the early Church did not favor it—perhaps because it was so closely identified with the excesses of the Romans. Cultivation practically ceased except for in a few monastery gardens until the time of Charlemagne. Even

◀ *Razzle Dazzle (floribunda).*

Courtesy of Sturbridge Village Library

Rosa alba *From Gerald's* **Herbal.** *One of the earliest roses brought to the settlers' gardens.*

after that, roses were mainly used as a medicinal. Not until the 1200s did roses once more become widespread and appreciated. Ironically, the Church then adapted the rose as a religious symbol—the white rose became the symbol for the Immaculate Conception of the Virgin Mary, and the briar rose (red in color) became a symbol of Christ's blood. A literal translation of the word *rosary* is "gathering of roses." The rose also became a popular design motif for the heraldic banners of many English noblemen. In 1272 Edward I used the rose design as his emblem. Over a century and a half later, the conflict between the British House of York, which took the white rose as its symbol, and the House of Lancaster, symbolized by the red rose, resulted in the War of the Roses (1455-85).

The China rose arrived in England and France from the Orient in 1789, and attracted many followers. In contrast to most roses, the China rose bloomed over a period of many months. Also from the Orient, the tea rose is a close relative of the China rose. The tea and China roses are the sources of our wonderful present-day hybrid teas (which are described in more detail on pp. 47-57).

Roses reached a peak of popularity in courtly Europe with Empress Josephine's grand palace and garden. The Empress's attempt to cultivate every known rose variety greatly influenced the popularity of roses and encouraged the development of new varieties. The Malmaison collection included gallicas, damasks, centifolias, Chinas, teas, Noisette roses (small shrub climbers), Bourbon, moss, and rugosa roses, plus others.

Roses occupy a prominent position in American history: American Indians were cultivating wild roses in the James River Valley when Captain John Smith established Jamestown in 1607, and the Pilgrims planted roses of their own in 1621. By 1722 the rose had found its way to our currency, embellishing the Rosa Americana coin with a five-petaled bloom; in 1856 a Kansas territorial bank issued a three-dollar bill festooned with roses and cupids. Roses have been grown on the White House grounds since John Adams planted some in what is now known as the Rose Garden. Today, the rose is the national floral emblem of America, as established by Congress and the President in 1986.

The rose will no doubt retain its popularity for years to come, for there are few flowers that match its form, color, grace, and elegance. It is truly the queen of flowers.

1 *Your Rose Garden*

Roses are really every gardener's flower; there simply is not another group of plants that provides such a variety of uses in a garden. They are the premier ornamental plant because they can be used as shrubs, climbers, hedges, color accent on arbors and along fences, or for borders. Roses can even be used as ground covers. In addition to their versatility in the garden, roses make superb cut flowers.

The main types of roses include hybrid teas, polyanthas, floribundas, grandifloras, climbers, ramblers, miniatures, old garden roses, and shrub roses. The large-flowered climbers, which can reach heights of twenty feet, are perfect for fences and walls (these roses bloom once a year), as are the ramblers, which have smaller flowers than the climbers. (Consult Chapter 3 for more information on these types of roses.) The old garden roses include all classes of roses in existence before 1867, including gallicas, damasks, albas, centifolias, moss roses, China and tea roses, Bourbons, and hybrid perpetuals. The miniatures are small replicas of the hybrid tea rose; some of the very smallest—with flowers less than an inch across—are called macro-miniatures. (Old garden roses and miniatures are covered in more detail in Chapter 3.) Shrub roses are sturdy, upright plants that, botanically, are neither old garden roses, nor members of any of the modern classes. They are a rather catch-all group of wild species, hybrids, and climbers that are usually hardy, disease- and pest-resistant.

Hybrid teas, grandifloras, and floribundas are the most commonly grown classes. Hybrid teas are a cross between hybrid

◀ *Saratoga (floribunda).*

5

Ann Reilly

Eclipse (hybrid tea).

perpetuals and tea roses, creating roses in a wide range of color and with long blooming seasons. Grandifloras are a cross between hybrid teas and floribundas, and are known for their vigor and high flower production. Floribundas are a cross between polyanthas and hybrid teas, and produce great quantities of flowers in clusters. The polyanthas are small plants that bear large clusters of small flowers.

Just how you use roses depends upon your garden's available space, its site and exposures, and various other factors. Floribundas and miniatures, for example, are excellent for raised beds or patio plantings; grandifloras make handsome hedges, and hybrid teas (everyone's favorite) excel in those areas where you need a touch of elegance, or where you want to make a bold statement of color. Ramblers and climbers are highly decorative, creating an old English cottage look. Roses can make a garden appear elegant or informal; they can impart an old-time ambience of leisure or a bright colorful note. Here are some basic points you should know about these classes. Chapter 3 discusses each in greater detail.

Why are the hybrid teas so popular?

Hybrid teas are favored for their large, many-petaled blooms produced singly on long stems. Though they need winter protection in the colder zones, they will bloom consistently in almost all climates.

Do the hybrid teas have the best color range of flowers?

Yes. Until 1900 hybrid teas were very limited in color—they were usually yellow. Now countless colors are available, including many tones of red, orange, yellow, lavender, and white.

Is the hybrid tea's flower form superior to other types of roses?

As a rule, yes. The stems are straight, the buds narrow, and the flowers elegant.

What is the season of bloom for hybrid teas?

From early summer until frost.

Are the hybrid teas as popular in other countries as they are in the United States?

They are the most widely grown rose today.

Can you briefly explain what kind of roses polyanthas are?

Polyanthas are a cross between the Japanese rose, *R. multiflora* and the China rose, *R. Chinensis*. They are low-growing, hardy plants bearing flowers over a long period of bloom.

Is the culture of polyanthas any more difficult than the culture of other roses?

No. In fact, they will thrive in many parts of the country where hybrid teas would do poorly.

What is the color range of the polyanthas?

They produce flowers of almost every color to be found among roses.

The main types or classes of roses.

What is the season of bloom for polyanthas?

Late spring through fall.

SHRUB ROSE

GRANDIFLORA

LARGE-FLOWERED CLIMBER

HYBRID TEA

RAMBLER

POLYANTHA

MINIATURE

Little Darling (floribunda).

What is the best use for polyanthas in a garden?

They are most often used in bed plantings, grouped together with plants of similar variety for a mass color effect.

Are floribunda roses large or small growers?

Floribundas have a low-growing habit, reaching two to three feet.

Are there any good reasons to grow floribundas rather than the popular hybrid teas?

Floribundas come into bloom a bit later than hybrid teas, but bloom in much greater profusion once they get going. Also, floribundas are hardier than the hybrid teas, which lack the ability to go dormant in cold weather and thus protect themselves from injury.

Is the color range among the floribundas as good as the hybrid teas'?

Yes, the flowers come in a wide range of colors—white, yellow, coral, pink, red, and lavender.

Do floribunda flowers grow singly?

No, the flowers are borne in huge clusters, creating a concentration of color.

Would you say the floribundas are ideal for cut flowers?

No, not like the hybrid teas. But many people do use them as cut flowers. They have good lasting quality.

Why are the grandifloras popular?

The grandifloras inherited their straight stems and elegant flower form from the hybrid teas, and their hardiness and flower clusters from the floribundas. They are, however, not hardy enough to withstand harsh winters.

Are the grandiflora flowers as large as the hybrid tea flowers?

No, they fall midway between the hybrid tea flower size and the floribunda's.

Are the grandifloras big plants?

They can grow quite tall, to six feet or more. They make handsome background plants for low-growing perennials of compatible colors.

What is the color range of the grandifloras?

Many tones of red, white, pink, orange, and some yellows.

Are the grandifloras as hardy as the hybrid teas?

Yes, even more so.

Camelot (grandiflora).

Ann Reilly

BASIC REQUIREMENTS FOR ROSE CULTIVATION

Roses have basic requirements for blooming. If you cannot meet these needs, it's better to grow something else. Try to envision what your garden will look like in a few years. This is especially important because roses do not like to be moved; you should never disturb their roots if you can help it. Many people make the mistake of planting just anywhere. Roses need fertilizing, pruning, and other ministrations, so create a convenient layout, one that leaves room for you to get to your plants in the future when they have grown larger.

I want to grow roses, but drainage is poor in the spot where I plan to put them. Any help?

Sure. Do a little drain work first. Dig trenches twenty inches deep and sloping away from the planting area. Fill them with a two-inch bed of gravel, and put soil over the bed. For cases of severely poor drainage, install drainage tiles. These four- or five-inch drain pipes, set about twenty-four inches below ground level, drain off excess water. (Chapter 2 discusses drainage further.)

Is it true that roses do not want other plants near them? If so, why?

Roses like the soil to themselves and do not want tree and shrub roots sneaking into their territory and draining away nutrients and moisture. Roses are not able to compete successfully with tree roots for soil nutrients.

How can I plant roses in a way that will make them easy to care for?

Allow space on two sides of the plantings if you can. The rose bed should be wide enough so that you can easily reach the plants from both sides. Stagger the plantings so that the bushes don't form a straight line.

What is the rule of thumb for spacing roses?

Hybrid teas and grandifloras should be about twenty-eight to thirty inches apart; where there is little or no frost, forty inches is better. Floribundas do well twenty-four inches apart—thirty inches in mild climates. Ramblers, shrub roses, and old garden roses need to be forty-eight to sixty inches apart.

My garden is plagued by wind; can I grow roses?

Yes you can, but be sure to water more often than you normally would.

Is a few hours of sun sufficient for roses?

Most roses like plenty of sun—at least four hours a day. Many types will grow well in less sunlight, though they will not bloom as often.

What climate conditions are not conducive to rose growing?

Roses will grow in almost any climate if they are of a species suited to local conditions. It is safe to say that many varieties will perform well in zones 4 through 7, and that the extremely hardy varieties will do well in zones 2 and 3 (see map, page 122). Roses can take a good deal of cold if the drop in temperature is gradual. (For information on winter protection methods, see Chapter 5.)

PLANNING YOUR ROSE GARDEN

Do not plant haphazardly when you begin to use roses in your garden. Make a few rough sketches to see what pleases you and what does not look proper in the overall scheme of things. Quick sketches are enough; you do not have to hire a landscape planner.

I have a small garden. Where is the best place for roses? What kind should I use?

Ideally, roses want a spot with at least four to six hours of daily sun; they do not prosper in shade.

Can I use roses in a terraced garden?

Yes, and with great drama. Plant several to a bed, with tall growers in the back, medium growers up front. Keep the plants well trimmed and they will create a handsome stairstep of color.

A stream of flowers spills down this terraced planting bed.

Maggie Oster

I have a rectangular yard; where might I place roses in my landscape plan?

In the total landscape plan try planting roses in one corner as an accent area, and repeat the accent with a drift (curve) of roses at the opposite end of the garden.

My yard is pie-shaped. Where should I put roses?

At the area along a fence or boundary line. Try using grandifloras, and keep them at a distance from the house for viewing pleasure.

How can I use roses to create a formal effect in my yard?

Put them in geometrically shaped beds, one bed mirroring the other. Do not concentrate more than four beds in one garden unless the area is extremely large.

My neighbor has landscaped her garden with large planter boxes. Will roses work in this situation?

Better than you might think. In large planter boxes, roses can impart a sense of completeness to a garden scene. In container gardens, they become the accent. (See the discussion of growing roses in containers in Chapter 2.)

If roses are so wonderful in landscape plans, why aren't they used more often?

In almost all parts of the country roses are becoming more popular garden plants as new insect- and disease-resistant varieties are being introduced. Today anyone can grow roses, whereas years ago there was a battle with the bugs. I believe we will see more and more roses in home gardens in future years.

SELECTING AND PURCHASING ROSES

Selecting roses is easy because there are roses for almost any situation, and the flowers come in so many colors. Base your selection on where the plants will be grown and how they will be part of the total landscape. Consider where the trees, shrubs, bulbs, flower beds, and so forth will be, and then select the appropriate roses. Choose colors that will create the garden you want. For instance, red is always vibrant and will stand out, but if you have many white flowers in the garden, red roses may create an excessive contrast. Use golden yellows and pinks with white, or try white roses. A careful blend of colors is vital in rose selection: do not plant yellow roses next to red ones unless you want to create a carnival atmosphere in the garden. White and yellow roses next to each other have a soft, graceful appeal.

There are a few things you should know when you shop for roses. The individual plants are graded for quality: No. 1, No. 1½, No. 2, and No. 3. Rose plants are available at many outlets now, including supermarkets, nurseries, and mail-order companies. Buying at your local nursery is best because you will receive personal help there if a plant fails to thrive. Mail-order buying is also fine. Many mail-order companies specialize in roses and depend solely on them for their business, so they strive to deliver the best—and usually do.

Are there bargains in roses?

You get what you pay for. Cheap roses may be of poor grade and not worth the trouble of planting. Always buy the best plants you can afford.

What is the best buy in grades?

Two-year-old, field-grown, No. 1 grade is always a good investment.

What are the major categories of rose colors as designated by the American Rose Society?

The colors are white or near white; medium yellow, deep yellow, yellow blend; light pink, medium pink, pink blend, deep pink; medium red, dark red, red blend; apricot blend; orange and orange blend; orange-red; russet; mauve, lavender.

Are the roses that are sold in supermarkets of good quality?

They may or may not be. Look for fresh canes on green, stout, and robust-looking plants. Avoid unhealthy-looking bargain roses.

There are so many roses at nurseries. How do I know which ones are best?

Decide what you want the roses for—bedding, background, color accent, indoor growing, whatever. Then choose the specific variety recommended for that particular need from the charts in this book (Chapter 3).

Is it all right to buy from mail-order suppliers?

Absolutely. These people specialize in roses, and offer the widest selection.

When is the best time to buy roses?

When they appear at your local nursery, which depends on where you live.

What are the easiest roses to grow?

The varieties Charlotte Armstrong, Duet, Granada, King's Ransom, Lady X, Peace, and Queen Elizabeth are all known for their robust growing habits.

Ann Reilly

Number 1 grade roses must be two years old when they are dug from the field, and must have at least three strong canes.

I live in a hot, dry climate. What varieties of roses do you suggest?

Charlotte Armstrong is a strong performer in such conditions, as are Granada, Mr. Lincoln, and Peace.

My climate is somewhat cool. Any rose suggestions?

Sure. Double Delight, Peace, Pascali, and Fragrant Cloud should all perform with gusto.

I want roses to cut. Which are the best?

There are so many that it is hard to recommend specific ones. However, you will not be disappointed by Camelot, Olé, Peace, Royal Highness, or the wonderful Tiffany.

Why is color in rose selection stressed so much?

Because selecting the colors you like helps to make a garden your very own. If yellow is your favorite color, use yellow roses, perhaps complementing them with white and apricot roses.

I want to use roses for a hedge effect. Which should I choose?

There are many good shrub beauties, but I prefer Bonica, Carefree Beauty, Europeana, and Simplicity.

I need ground cover–type roses. Which ones are best?

Ralph's Creeper, *Rosa wichuraiana,* and Sea Foam do fine as ground covers, but any of the miniature roses will work well, too.

I want a fragrant rose garden. What are the best roses for scent?

Chrysler Imperial, Fragrant Cloud, Perfume Delight, Granada, Sutter's Gold, and Tiffany have wonderful scents.

Ann Reilly

Double Delight.

CLASSIFICATION OF ROSE TYPES

Plant groups can be confusing: there are species, hybrids, cultivars, and varieties. Serious collectors need to know a rose's parentage, but for the rest of us, a cursory acquaintance with the various classes and names is sufficient.

The rose family contains 150 or more species, or types, of roses. These roses all have certain characteristics in common. The species roses are wild; from these plants come all the other roses, which are hybrids. *Hybridization* is breeding two plants to produce a new plant that retains some characteristics from both parent plants. In nature, bees and other insects randomly perform the hybridization process via cross-pollination. Humans hybridize plants to produce larger flowers, better form, resistance to disease, and other desirable characteristics.

The results of the different species crosses are called varieties; the varieties created by humans are named cultivars. Varieties or cultivars may also occur as *sports,* chance genetic mutations of nature. When a human-created rose is ready for the market, it needs a cultivar name, so the hybridizer selects a name and registers it with the American Rose Society. The registration center reviews the name of the plant and its description, rejecting it if it does not meet the provisions of the International Code (for example, if the name already exists or is too similar to one already registered).

PLANT PATENTS

Today, a hybridizer can patent a specific rose. The patent gives the hybridizer, who may have spent years and much money developing the plant, a certain remuneration for every offspring of the plant that is produced. It is an infringement of the Patent Act to reproduce patented roses while the patent protecting them is in force. Some rose nurseries purchase licenses from developers to propagate and sell specific roses.

By law, patented plants must carry metal tags and be numbered. The metal tag attached to the plant guarantees that the plant will be the cultivar it is advertised to be.

ROSE RATINGS

The All-America Rose Selections (AARS) are the best of the new varieties each year. The AARS system was established fifty years ago when over twenty official test gardens were set up throughout the United States, many at universities and public rose gardens. Roses are tested at these gardens for two years and rated in many categories. The judges look for novelty, bud form, flower form, color at opening, color at finishing, substance, vigor, and growth habit. Plants are distributed to 135 public rose gardens the year before they are listed in the catalog so they can be observed during the blooming season.

Every year members of the American Rose Society (ARS) rate hundreds of new roses, and the annually published *Handbook for Selecting Roses* carries the listings. Rose growers are asked to vote for new roses on a scale of 1 to 10. The results are averaged, and after a rose has been rated for five years, a national rating for that rose is proclaimed. The ARS rose rating is important because it gives an indication of how a rose will perform. Here are the ARS ratings:

Perfect	10
Superior	9.9-9.0
Very good	8.9-8.0
Good	7.9-7.0
Average	6.9-6.0
Poor	5.9-5.0
Very poor	4.9

A low-rated rose may be suitable in some situations. For example, if you like fragrance or color, a 7.9 rose might be fine for you because it happens to be your favorite color and has a pleasing fragrance.

Just what does all this rose testing mean to me?

It assures you that you are getting the best roses available. The very good is separated from the very bad. It does *not* mean that you shouldn't select a plant with a lower rating if you like, but you will be aware of your selection's shortcomings.

For the sake of a rose beginner such as I am, can you explain the meaning of the AARS categories?

Here are two examples. Bud form refers to the quality of a bud's basic shape, which may be slender or tapered, pointed, ovoid, urn-shaped, or rounded. Substance—the texture of the petals as determined by the amount of moisture and starch in them—is vital, because it gives a rose its vibrancy and color.

What about color and fragrance in a rose? I thought they were the prime considerations. Aren't they?

Yes they are, to some people. Let us take color first. People choose roses by color more than any other attribute. But colors vary. Red is not simply red; it might be dark, light, or in between. A rose you select from a catalog for its color may produce a different shade when you plant it in your region, depending on the weather and cultural conditions. And fragrance is a very personal thing—what is sweet-smelling to you

Ann Reilly

Gene Boerner (floribunda).

DISEASE RESISTANCE

There is no guarantee that the following roses are disease resistant; only that they have a better chance of avoiding disease than some other roses.

Bonica
Carousel
Chicago Peace
Confidence
Evening Star
First Prize
Miss All-American Beauty
Mr. Lincoln
Peace

Pink Parfait
Pink Peace
Queen Elizabeth
Razzle Dazzle
Rose Parade
Shreveport
Sonia
Tiffany

Derek Fell

Queen Elizabeth (hybrid tea).

may be too heavy a scent for another person. Select a rose fragrance that pleases you. Roses have spicy scents, heavy aromas, delicate fragrances, citrus scents, and so on.

Is it stupid to buy a poorly rated rose, say one rated "Good" quality?

No, not if it has some special attribute you personally like. I would, however, avoid "Poor" graded roses.

What are the names of some very good roses to buy?

The best thing to do is to choose from among your personal favorites or the All-America Rose Selections winners.

Do all the rose growers have their own award-winning roses?

Yes, they do. And even if a particular rose does not win an award, it might be a recent introduction, so it always pays to get catalogs from companies. (Some are listed at the end of the book.)

What were some of the high-rated roses during the past few years?

Hybrid teas: Peace (8.9), First Prize (9.1), Tiffany (8.3), Supersprite (8.9), and Tropicana (8.6). *Floribundas:* Europeana (9.1), Little Darling (8.8), and Iceberg (8.9). *Grandifloras:* Queen Elizabeth (9.1) and Sonia (8.1). *Miniatures:* Starina (9.6). *Climbers:* Dortmund (9.2).

What are your personal favorites?

Peace and Royal Highness are my favorite teas. In the grandiflora class I cannot resist Queen Elizabeth. My floribunda selection is Gene Boerner. Here are some further recommendations to help you make your rose selections:

Ann Reilly

Tiffany (hybrid tea).

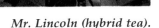

Mr. Lincoln (hybrid tea).

Roses for Special Places and Purposes

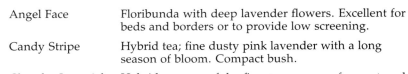

NAME	COMMENTS
FRAGRANCE	
Angel Face	Floribunda with deep lavender flowers. Excellent for beds and borders or to provide low screening.
Candy Stripe	Hybrid tea; fine dusty pink lavender with a long season of bloom. Compact bush.
Chrysler Imperial	Hybrid tea; one of the finest roses; very fragrant, red flowers; upright growth, winter hardy, disease resistant, but mildew-prone in cool, moist climates. All-America Rose Selection for 1953.
Fragrant Cloud	Hybrid tea; tough to beat for its brilliant red color. Tall grower to 4 feet; excellent for a strong garden statement.
Mr. Lincoln	Hybrid tea; vigorous grower, large red flowers. A very popular rose and an All-America Rose Selection for 1965.
Saratoga	Floribunda; very large white flowers, long bloomer. Good hedge plant.
Spartan	Floribunda; lovely orange-red flowers, well-favored by many. Introduced in 1955 and winner of several gold medals.
Tropicana	Hybrid tea; one of the world's favorite roses. Beautiful orange-coral flowers used frequently as cut flowers because blooms last a long time. All-America Rose Selection for 1963.
CUT FLOWERS	
Charlotte Armstrong	Hybrid tea; the veteran of many rose shows and winner of many gold medals. Beautiful pink flowers are borne profusely over long season.
Chicago Peace	Hybrid tea; pink-and-yellow, elegant-shaped flowers. Grows in compact bush and has strong straight stems. Excellent.

Chicago Peace (hybrid tea).

Roses for Special Places and Purposes
(continued)

NAME	COMMENTS
First Prize	Hybrid tea; very large, deep rose flowers. Upright vigorous plant with strong stems and attractive foliage. All-America Rose Selection in 1970.
Granada	Hybrid tea; very large 3- to 5-inch red-yellow flowers. Urn-shaped buds. Award-winning for its fragrance.
Pascali	Hybrid tea; creamy white, double flowers with superb shape. Vigorous, and has few thorns. Highly prized.
Queen Elizabeth	Grandiflora; pink flowers 3½ to 4 inches across. The original and probably most famous grandiflora rose. Almost thornless, and winner of many gold medals.
Tiffany	Hybrid tea; pink and gold 4- to 5-inch flowers. A real show-stopper. Vigorous, and blooms profusely.
White Masterpiece	Hybrid tea; large (6-inch) white flowers, beautifully shaped. Vigorous. A favorite.

GROUND COVER

Max Graf	Shrub rose; lovely 3-inch pink flowers. A true trailer type to about 2 feet. Blooms once in spring or in early summer.
New Dawn	Large-flowered climber; fine pink flowers. Abundant bloom. Vigorous, it can grow to 20 feet.
Dortmund	Climber; famous white-centered red rose. Long trailing canes to 10 feet. May be used as a ground cover if canes are held close to the ground with pegs.

LOW HEDGES

Betty Prior	Floribunda; small 2- to 3-inch pink flowers. Plants grow to about 4 feet. One of the best of the older roses.
Cathedral	Floribunda; 3-inch salmon flowers. Handsome color accent, attractive foliage.
Frau Dagmar Hartopp (Hastrup)	Shrub rose; beautiful pink 2-to 3-inch flowers. Grows to about 5 feet, blooms over a long season. Very popular.
The Fairy	Polyantha; clusters of small pink flowers that bloom abundantly for many months. Grows to about 2 feet
Trumpeter	Floribunda; bright red flowers in large clusters. Grows to about 2 feet.

TALL ROSES

F.J. Grootendorst	Shrub rose; very small red flowers. Blooms in spring and again in fall. Grows tall, to 7 feet.
Golden Wings	Shrub rose; 4-inch single yellow flowers. Very vigorous, growing to 7 feet. Introduced in 1936 and still a favorite.
Sparrieshoop	Shrub rose; pink 4-inch flowers. Plants bloom in spring and fall; grows to 12 feet.
Queen Elizabeth	Grandiflora; pink 3½- to 4-inch flowers. Blooms in abundance in midseason. Fragrant. Winter hardy and disease resistant. Grows 5 to 7 feet.

Betty Prior (floribunda).

Golden Wings (shrub rose).

2 *Successful Rose Growing*

There are no tricks to growing roses, nor is there any more work involved in cultivating the "queen of flowers" than a bed of petunias; but certain nutrients must be available and certain procedures must be in order if the plants are to thrive. The basic building block is food, which means soil.

Watering, fertilizing, and pruning enter the picture as well, but these elements are easily provided, even by the sometimes neglectful gardener. The basic rules are easy to follow: Prepare the soil in advance, plant the roses at the proper depth, fertilize them on a regular schedule, and prune them at the proper times. The result will be successful rose growing, even for the novice.

PLANTING BARE-ROOT ROSES

The initial planting of roses is important. The holes you dig in the ground must be deep enough for the plants—a minimum of 18 inches—and bare-root stock should be soaked in a bucket of water for several hours before being planted. Put bare-root roses (those not in containers when purchased) into the ground when they are available at local nurseries or mail-order suppliers. Roses bought in containers do not need to be soaked first, and can be planted at almost any time during clement weather. (We will discuss container-grown roses in the next section.)

When is the best time to plant roses?

This varies throughout the United States, but generally, in very cold climates, roses are planted in early spring. In the South, Southwest, and on the West Coast, roses are planted in

◀ *Confidence (hybrid tea).*

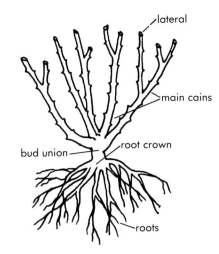

Anatomy of a bare-root rose.

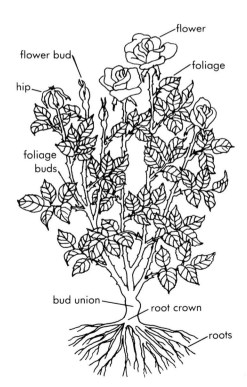

Anatomy of a rose bush.

January or February. To be safe, plant roses when they become available at your local nurseries.

Can't roses be planted at any other time of the year?

Roses can be planted in the fall in climates that do not have extremely cold winters.

How deep should roses be put into the ground?

Make holes fifteen to eighteen inches wide and deep.

How exactly do I plant roses?

Before planting your new rose, completely submerge the roots and canes in a tub of water for two hours. Meanwhile dig a hole and refill it partially with a mound of loose soil mixed with a quart of peat moss or other organic matter. Remove the plant from the water and trim away any broken or withered sections of roots and canes. Now gently spread the roots and arrange them in a natural manner on this pyramid of soil. Make sure the level of the soil is slightly above the bud union. Add soil around the roots, packing it down with your hands every so often and finally tamping it with your feet when all the soil is in. Water thoroughly to settle the soil, wait a few moments, and then water the soil again.

If I follow your directions but the rose leans to one side, what should I do?

Do not try to straighten the plant by pushing it into erect alignment. Instead, dig out the soil and start again. It is essential that the rose start life properly erect, and that you meet all its cultural requirements.

Should I perform a soil test before I plant roses?

No. This is extra work, and even if the soil does not contain all the necessary ingredients, you will be adding the proper nutrients when you start fertilizing the plants.

What about determining proper pH?

Though slightly acid soil is ideal for roses, they will grow well in almost any soil. Test your soil if you really want to, or if you suspect a major pH imbalance, but a test is usually not necessary.

What should I do with the plastic bags or sheeting that covers the roses when they come from the nursery?

If you are going to hold the plants for a few days, remove any plastic covering material so moisture does not form inside. Heel them in as described on page 24.

PLANTING A BARE-ROOT ROSE

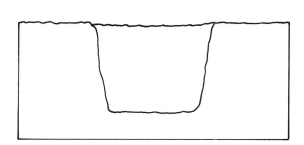

1. Soak the roots for a few hours; dig a hole.

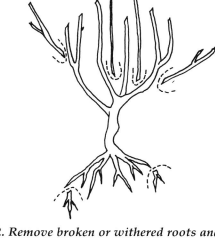

2. Remove broken or withered roots and canes.

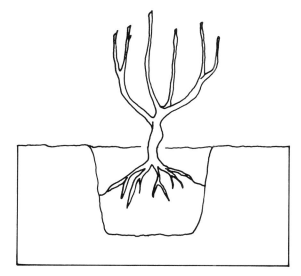

3. Spread the roots over the mound of soil.

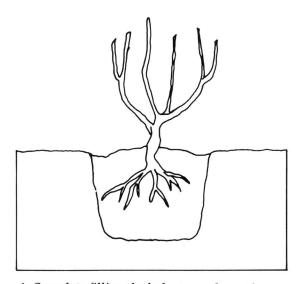

4. Complete filling the hole, tamp down the soil, and water thoroughly.

If I follow your advice but the rose refuses to grow after a time, what should I do?

Check the soil to be sure that moisture is getting to the roots. Dig out a small amount of soil to see how deep the water has penetrated. If the soil is dry beneath the surface, incorporate peat moss into it. If the plant still refuses to grow, take it out of the hole, prune the roots somewhat, cut the canes back to about four inches, and replant. Then hope for the best.

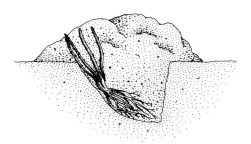

It is best to heel-in a bare-root rose if you are not going to plant it within a week or two.

PLANTING CONTAINER-GROWN ROSES

Do I have to plant the roses the same day I get them?

Yes, that is best; or plant them the next day. The point is to plant them as soon as possible so that they can begin growing again. If you have to let plants sit a week or so, "heel them in" in the following manner: Dig a shallow trench, lay the rose bushes on their sides with their roots in the trench, and cover the bushes with soil, canes and all. Water the plants lightly and keep them shaded. This procedure slows deterioration until the plants can be restored to their natural condition of growth.

In many areas of the country, people buy roses that have been grown in containers. If a rose you buy is in a can, have a nursery attendant slit the can for you. Then be sure to get the rose into the ground as soon as possible.

What is the advantage of a container-grown rose?

Some people say such a rose takes the shock of planting better than a bare-root specimen because the plant is already growing. Indeed, in some areas you can buy container-grown roses already in flower.

What are the advantages of bare-root plants?

They are available for planting at almost any time of the year, and they come in a much wider variety of cultivars than do container-grown roses. They are also less expensive.

What is the basic planting procedure for container-grown roses?

Gently loosen the rose from the container—do not pull the plant. Try to keep the rootball intact. Insert the rose into a previously dug, deep hole as previously discussed for bare-root roses, and follow that planting procedure.

How long does it take before a container-grown plant becomes well established?

A shorter time than it takes for a bare-root specimen: about three to four weeks.

How far up the base of the plant should I put soil?

The bud union should be at the depth as previously described for bare-root planting.

Can I buy all varieties of roses in containers?

I doubt it very much. Some roses are available only in containers, others only bare-root.

Ann Reilly

Remove the cardboard from a boxed rose, even if the label tells you to leave it on.

The soil in which you plant roses must be nutritionally complete. Roses will grow in poor soil, but this means a lot of stress and strain on the plants. Proper drainage is also vital because stagnant water at the roots will damage plants.

SOIL AND SOIL DRAINAGE

What is the best soil for roses?

The best soil drains readily and contains the proper nutrients. The soil should feel like a mealy baked potato when you handle it, and have a humusy, woodsy aroma. It should hold moisture, yet drain well.

What if my soil is dry and cakey?

Dig it up, thoroughly mix in some organic matter such as peat moss, aged manure, or compost, and let the soil "work" for a few weeks before the roses are planted.

Are there any shortcuts to creating good aerated soil?

Sure, if you have the money. Discard the old spent soil from the planting hole and fill it with rich topsoil from a nursery.

My soil is very sandy and not much grows for me. Will roses succeed in it?

Only with great effort on your and the plants' part. It is best to mix organic matter into the soil. Compost is ideal because it usually contains all of the major and most (if not all) of the minor plant nutrients. Also water during dry periods, and add fertilizer during the growing season.

What is the best organic matter for improving soil texture and drainage?

Commercially packaged peat moss improves texture and drainage; you can add up to one-half peat moss per volume of soil. Seasoned steer manure adds nutrients, too, as does leaf mold gathered from the woods.

How can I improve drainage in my soil?

You can aerate it as described above, or dig shallow trenches in a spider web-like arrangement so water can drain off quickly. You can also dig trenches twenty inches deep, fill them with gravel or pebbles, and cover the material with soil.

What happens if my roses do not get proper drainage?

They will not grow and bloom very well, though they will not die. If you don't want to put in drainage facilities, grow your plants in raised beds or in large planter boxes with drainage holes. The soil will drain readily this way.

WATERING AND DRIP SYSTEMS

It is necessary to water roses regularly during dry weather because they require even moisture in their soil. Too much dryness will impede their growth. Conversely, if the soil gets too mushy, drainage will be slowed and the roots will suffer. Remember that a rose plant is only as good as its roots.

The way you water your roses makes a difference, too. Sprinklers are hit-and-miss, and hand watering is a chore. The best watering system is a drip set-up. An automatic regulator controls the water so that the soil always receives the proper amount of moisture.

Summer mulching is a good way to reduce the necessity of supplemental watering. Straw, pebbles, plastic, humus, peanut hulls, or bark spread around the base of each plant will conserve moisture and reduce evaporation. Mulch also keeps rainwater from running off during downpours—an important precaution for sloping areas.

The depth of a mulch can be from two to six inches, depending on the density of the mulch and the amount of drought protection your roses need. Provide a layer that is deep enough to keep the soil from drying out, but not so deep that air and water do not reach the soil.

Apply mulch in early summer if you live in a drought area. Loosen the soil first with a hoe, soak it with water, and then apply the mulch. Some mulches, such as bark, humus, and pebbles, last for years (even pebbles eventually disappear if they're spread directly on the soil); others break down fast and need regular replacement. Mulching, especially when combined with a drip watering system, goes a long way in keeping your roses beautiful even if rain is scant. (For more information about mulching, see pp. 112-13.)

Ann Reilly

With this drip-watering system, plastic collars sunk a few inches into the ground hold the water within the root zone of the plant.

When is the best time to water roses?

Early morning suits the plants fine because they have all day to absorb the moisture and are dry by night, preventing mildew.

Do roses need much water?

Absolutely. Some experts swear by one inch of rainfall or irrigation per week.

Won't rainfall take care of watering?

No, and do not assume that it will. Remember, it takes at least three hours of rain to penetrate twenty-four inches of soil.

Why do roses need so much water?

Their roots must have moisture, and because rose roots are twenty-four inches or more below ground level, moistening the roots thoroughly takes plenty of water—five gallons at a watering would not be too much.

I don't have time to water my roses for very long. Can't I just give them a light hosing?

No. This does more harm than good because shallow watering makes roots have to work to find moisture, and consequently weakens the plants. If you don't have time to water your roses thoroughly, wait until the next day and do it right.

My neighbor says the proper amount of water for your roses depends on your soil. Is this true?

To a degree your neighbor is right. Different soils do require different amounts of water. But ideally you have prepared a proper soil, which will call for heavy watering.

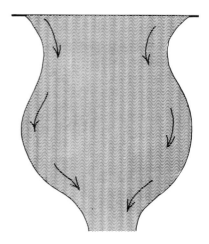

Water moves laterally—does not fan out to a significant degree.

DEPTH	COARSE SAND	SANDY LOAM	CLAY
0			
6"			
12"	15 minutes	30 minutes	60 minutes
18"			
24"		60 minutes	
30"	40 minutes		
36"			
42"			
48"	60 minutes		

Water descends rapidly through sandy soil and is soon lost. A clay soil, on the other hand, resists water penetration.

Won't too much water clog the soil and roots?

Yes. Roots need oxygen, and if the soil is muddy and saturated, oxygen cannot get to the roots. (But, as mentioned earlier, soil should be evenly moist—never soggy, never dry.)

Is there any sure-fire way of telling whether I am watering my roses properly?

Stick your fingers or hand down into the soil. If the soil is moderately damp and smells woodsy, you are doing the job right.

Do sprinkling systems supply the proper amount of water?

The systems spray water randomly, requiring you to waste time determining whether the water spray is hitting the root area. Sprinkling also wets the leaves, which can spread blackspot disease if the weather is overcast and cool.

Water systems appropriate for rose gardens.

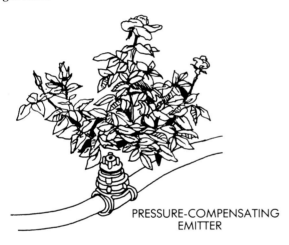

PRESSURE-COMPENSATING EMITTER

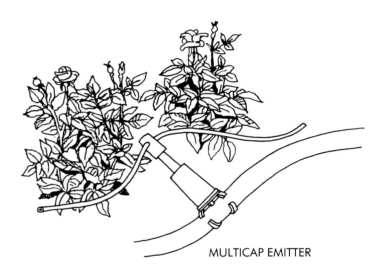

MULTICAP EMITTER

UNDERGROUND REED EMITTER

EXTENDED REED EMITTER

What is the best method of watering?

Without a doubt, drip watering does the job almost perfectly. It supplies water at a regulated rate so that the root system receives just the right amount of moisture. It also saves water by putting it only where it is needed. Water is a precious commodity, and should not be wasted. You can buy a drip irrigation kit at most any garden center.

Exactly how do I combine a mulch and a drip watering system?

Lay out the drip system first, and then spread the mulch over it. Push some mulch aside on occasion and test the ground beneath it to make sure that the roses are getting enough water.

Can't I just use a hose to water roses?

Sure, but remember to water thoroughly. It takes time to water a bush. You need about five gallons of water to penetrate the soil, which means several minutes holding the hose on each plant.

FERTILIZING

No matter how good (or how bad) your soil is, the plants growing in it will eventually require feeding so they can receive the nutrients they need. You can grow some roses without giving them food and they will survive, but most roses (hybrid teas, for example) simply do not thrive without proper fertilization.

The correct feeding involves the use of a liquid or powdered plant food that contains nitrogen, phosphorus, and potassium. These three elements supply almost all the nutrients necessary for plant growth. Nitrogen promotes leaf growth; phosphorus assists root development and flower formation; and potassium helps the plant manufacture sugars, which promote strong growth.

The various fertilizers on the market contain pretty much the same elements, but in different amounts. Some liquid plant foods, for example, contain 20 percent nitrogen, 20 percent phosphorus, and 10 percent potassium; their bottles will be marked 20-20-10. Other fertilizers may contain a 10-10-5 ratio, and so on.

You can also use organic fertilizers for roses: cottonseed meal, manures, bloodmeal, and bonemeal. Many growers supplement synthetic fertilizers with some organic ingredients. There are also fertilizers made specifically for roses.

How do I know the best type of plant food to use on my roses?

It is difficult to recommend one specific plant food. Generally, a food containing 10 percent nitrogen, 10 percent phosphorus, and 5 percent potassium works fine for most roses. Your best bet is to observe the plants and see how they do with a particular food. If they are growing well with one type, keep using it. If the plants seem to be slow-growing, or if their foliage is not a healthy green, try a different fertilizer.

Are liquid fertilizers better than powdered ones?

Either form is fine. Powdered foods are applied to the ground surface around the rose bush and watered in. Liquid fertilizers must first be mixed in water and then applied. If you have many roses, the powdered form of food might be better because it is easier to apply. For small gardens, liquid feeding is no chore.

Do brand names make a difference?

No, brand names are simply that—names. Also, foods made specifically for roses may not be much better than standard plant foods.

Is organic feeding—with manure and such—really necessary?

Yes. These naturally occurring nutrients are organic and so is your soil. They help keep the soil structure in a desirable condition. Organic foods do not become active until the soil warms up, so you run less risk of applying too much fertilizer at the wrong time. Use some organic food to get growth started, along with commercial fertilizers; that seems the best overall program.

When should I start fertilizing roses?

In early spring, after the first pruning. Fertilize newly planted roses after a few weeks, or after they've sent out several inches of new growth.

Is there any specific time for applying plant foods, such as morning or night?

The best time of day to apply foods is early morning. The soil should be moist, not dry. During the heat of the day plants can sometimes react adversely to plant foods.

How often should I use plant food?

A mild application every two to three weeks works for most roses. But again, this question can be answered only by observing the plants. Roses indicate whether they need more or less food by leaf color, bud formation, and overall appearance.

What feeding schedule do you recommend?

I feed roses twice a month with a liquid fertilizer, and once a month with a mild organic fertilizer such as cottonseed meal.

When should I stop feeding my roses?

Six to eight weeks before the first fall frost.

Do I need any special equipment for feeding roses?

No. You can mix liquid food in a bucket or watering can and apply the mixture to the soil. If you have very many roses, invest in a siphon hose attachment. Mix a bucketful of concentrated liquid plant food. Water flowing through the hose uses a measured amount of fertilizer through the siphon and dilutes it with water from the hose to the proper strength.

Are there any other directions for plant feeding that I should know?

Always follow the directions on the package or bottle of plant food to the letter. With plant feeding, more is not necessarily better.

I have heard a great deal about plant foods that contain both food and insect repellents. What are they?

Some plant foods also contain *systemic* insecticides. These chemicals will kill sucking insects for a time (about a month). However, the combination of insecticide and plant food is not really necessary and is an added expense.

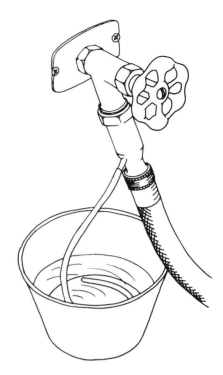

The siphon-bucket fertilizing method is simple and inexpensive.

PRUNING AND CUTTING

Roses like to grow, so eventually the time comes when you must prune them. Pruning is cutting and removing some growth, and there are varied opinions as to how much is suitable for roses. Some experts say prune hard—that is, cut away a great deal—whereas other rose people say to prune lightly. The best policy is to prune moderately; this way you take no risks with your plants. Although pruning sounds like work, it is not. You have to prune only at the end of the growing season (to accommodate winter protection methods, or to remove dead or damaged canes), or just before plants send out new growth.

You will need sturdy hand-pruning shears, and long-handled shears for thick canes. Buy the best tools you can afford, because cheap tools become useless within a year. I prefer wooden-handled, heavy-duty shears and pruning tools. A high quality pair of heavy gardening gloves is important, too.

What are the objectives of pruning?

To encourage new growth and remove damaged or dead wood. Pruning also helps roses maintain a handsome shape.

Just how much of the rose should I cut away?

About one-third of the past year's growth. The objective is to open up the bush by cutting away crossed and dead branches.

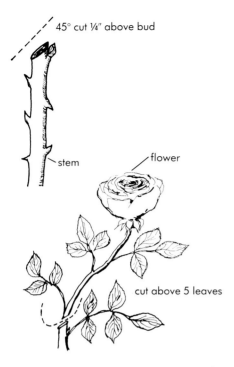

45° cut ¼" above bud

stem

flower

cut above 5 leaves

Proper cutting technique is essential to the health of your rose bush.

More drastic pruning is necessary in very cold climates to accommodate the type of winter protection your roses get.

Why are pruning tools so important?

Good sharp pruning shears make the task easy. They are also good for cutting flowers to bring indoors.

Is there a specific way to cut?

Make cuts at a 45-degree angle ¼ inch above an outside leaf bud. (See illustration.)

Is it all right to leave the cut open?

No. Paint large cuts with a sealing compound (sold at nurseries). If the cuts are on thin stems, no painting is necessary.

Should I prune all types of roses the same way?

No. Climbers, ramblers, and old garden roses require distinct methods. Do not prune big climbers and climbing teas for two years, until there is strong cane growth. Then remove only dead canes and flowers. Prune ramblers after their flowers have faded and new growth shows; cut away canes that have just flowered, and tie new canes to supports. Lightly prune old garden roses to thin and shape them.

What is disbudding?

Some gardeners, wanting fine cut flowers, pinch out the side buds while they are still very tiny. This is generally done only on hybrid teas.

In the spring, prune: 1) dead, damaged, or diseased canes; 2) old canes that have been replaced by new ones; 3) suckers, which start below the bud union; 4) canes and twigs to maintain the proper shape of the bush.

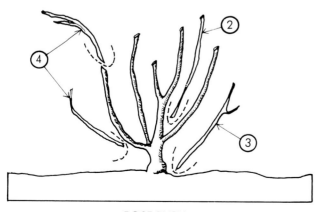

ROSE BUSH

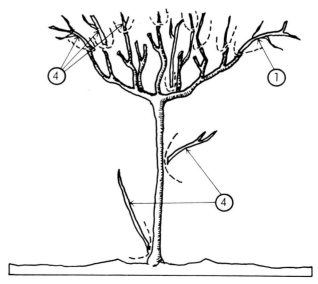

ROSE TREE

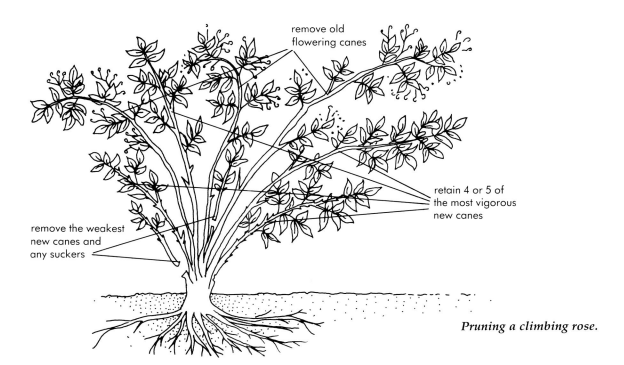

remove old
flowering canes

retain 4 or 5 of
the most vigorous
new canes

remove the weakest
new canes and
any suckers

Pruning a climbing rose.

How should I prune shrub roses?

Shrub roses are best left to develop their natural shape. Thin them out and remove old or tangled canes after the flowers have stopped blooming. The types that spread by surface or underground suckers need persistent pruning to prevent them from growing rampant and forming clumps or thickets.

I have heard that suckers on roses need to be cut away. Is this true?

Yes, this is recommended. The trouble is that it is sometimes difficult to recognize a sucker (see illustration, above). It usually looks different from the regular growth; it may be long and spindly, for example. Pull the sucker down and tear it from the plant. Cutting it may leave growth eyes at the base, which will produce more suckers.

How exactly should I prune hybrid teas?

The hybrid teas, floribundas, and grandifloras are all pruned the same way. Cut away twiggy branches and dead wood, and try to open the center of the bush by removing excess growth. Cut away almost one-half of the growth that was made during the year, but do not remove any thick-caned growth.

Can you give me the details of how to prune climbers?

Leave a hybrid tea climber alone for two years after its initial planting so that it can become well established with strong canes. Remove only twiggy growth and dead canes. As the canes mature, tie them into position against a fence, post, or other support. When the climber has thick, strong, long canes, smaller branches will grow out and bear the flowers. Do not cut away any long canes unless they are damaged and not producing, in which case prune them down to the ground. Remember that the long canes on climbers produce the laterals for flowering. For yearly pruning, remove only the old canes and prune the laterals, leaving two to three eyes. Treat the large-flowered climbers the same way for the first two to three years. Those climbers that produce flowers just once a year should be pruned after their bloom. Cut away weak, unproductive canes and any twiggy, weak branches. Prune the large-flowering climbers that bloom on-and-off from spring until fall the same way you do hybrid teas.

Which are the best pruning shears?

There are two types of pruning shears. The scissors-type shears have two cutting edges passing each other; the anvil type has a cutting blade that presses down against a flat bed. Anvil shears are more durable than the scissors type because the blades of the scissors can be forced apart in cutting.

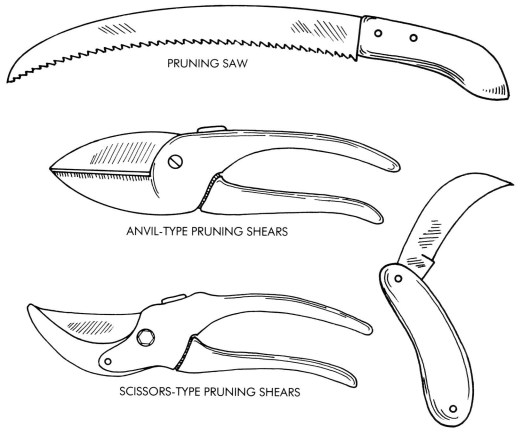

PRUNING SAW

ANVIL-TYPE PRUNING SHEARS

SCISSORS-TYPE PRUNING SHEARS

POCKETKNIFE

Pruning tools.

I have an old tree saw. Will this work to prune my roses?

No. Use a crescent-shaped, medium-size pruning saw to make neat cuts on canes.

Do I need any power tools for pruning roses?

No, none at all.

I have always used a pocketknife to cut roses. Is this all right?

Yes, if you keep the knife clean and sharp. Use one with an extra strong blade.

What is the best way to keep pruning tools clean?

Always scrape dirt and debris from your tools immediately after using them. Work the tools into a bucket of sand to remove any remaining dirt, and keep the blades sharp and free of rust.

Can I use these same tools for pruning and cutting miniature roses?

No. For the miniatures, a pair of small hand-pruning shears is fine. Use household scissors for cutting roses.

TRANSPLANTING

Transplanting is a shock to any established rose shrub, so try to avoid the moving process. However, sometimes a mature rose gets crowded out by other plants or is not exactly where you thought you wanted it when you planted it, so transplanting is needed. This is best done in early spring or late fall. Prune the bush first, leaving three to four canes. Prepare the new hole in the ground and proceed as you would with a fresh plant, but give it some extra attention after it is planted, and observe how it is faring. With luck, the transplant should work.

Will I kill a rose by transplanting it?

No, but you should transplant at the proper time and prune the rose to three or four canes before moving it. As a precaution, propagate new plants from cuttings of a valued rose bush a year before transplanting it.

Is spring the best time to transplant a rose?

Yes, definitely, because warm weather is on the way. The plant has a good chance of starting into a new period of growth.

Exactly how should I uproot a rose to move it?

Prune away one-third of the shrub, or enough to keep the top and roots in proportion. Dig a trench twelve inches from the crown all around the shrub. Use your shovel to remove soil from around the plant, then push down on the shovel handle to loosen the root ball. Finally, grasp the crown of the plant with your hands (wearing gloves) and push it to and fro until it is quite loose. Lift it out of its hole with the shovel.

After I have the plant out of the ground, should I take any precautions?

Examine the roots. Cut away any that are shriveled or dead (blackish).

TRANSPLANTING A ROSE

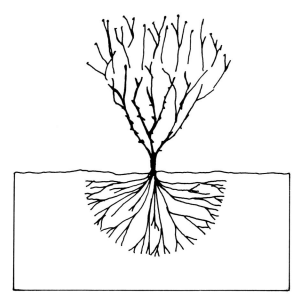

1. Prune one-third of the shrub.

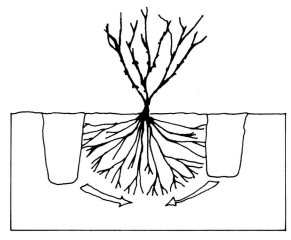

2. Dig trenches to remove the root ball.

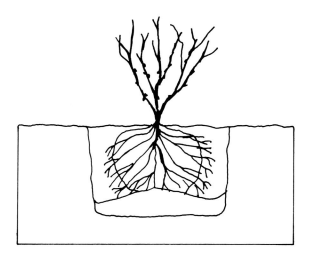

3. Add two inches of compost, build a mound of soil, and spread the roots over it.

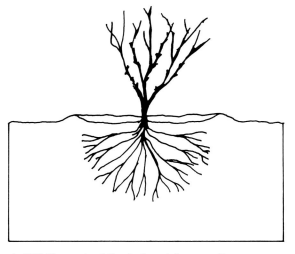

4. Fill the rest of the hole with topsoil, create a ridge of soil around the base of the plant, and water thoroughly.

How should I plant the moved rose?

Use the same method as you would for a new rose. Dig a deep hole and fill it with soil after you have centered the plant. Water well.

Should I use rooting powder?

A slight dusting of hormone powder, available at garden centers, will not hurt. It helps the plant reestablish itself.

What care does the plant need after it has been transplanted?

Water carefully at first, and make sure the rose is responding. Too much water can harm the plant because it clogs the soil and prevents air from reaching the roots. If a plant does not get enough water, it may starve. Remember, you moved the plant so it needs a little coddling.

How will I know if the transplanting process did not work?

The plant will have limp leaves and wilted stems.

Is there any other time of the year when I can transplant a rose?

Winter would be the other time. Some people recommend this because they believe that a plant in its dormant stage has a better chance of recovering from the shock of transplanting. I have always successfully moved roses in early spring.

GROWING ROSES IN CONTAINERS

Roses make fine container plants as long as they receive closer attention than you would give garden roses. Routine watering, good light, and regular feeding are essential. Plant the shrubs in large tubs (at least eighteen inches across and twenty-four inches deep), and do not disturb them for many years. In smaller pots or boxes, roots get cramped and growth is hindered.

Growing in containers has many advantages. The roses have the soil to themselves, with no competition from other plants; if your garden soil is bad, you can provide fresh new soil with adequate nutrients; you can (with some help) move the planter boxes or containers around.

What kind of container should I grow roses in?

Wooden tubs and boxes are excellent because the soil in them stays cool, and moisture can evaporate through the wood. Be sure that the tubs and boxes have drainage holes.

Can I use plastic containers?

Avoid them. Plastic containers heat up in the sun, so roots on the heated side of the container can die.

TRANSPLANTING A CONTAINER-GROWN ROSE

1. Remove the root ball from the container.

2. Trim away one to two inches of soil, being careful not to damage the roots.

3. Place the rose in the new container and fill the empty space with fresh soil; water.

Maggie Oster

Old wine or whiskey barrels make lovely patio planters.

Can I plant either bare-root or container-grown roses in boxes?

Container-grown stock does best in boxes and planters because the roots have been accustomed to growing in close quarters. Bare-root roses can adapt too, but they take longer to come around.

What kind of growing medium should I use for roses in containers?

Use a mixture of three parts sandy garden loam to one part peat moss. You may use a commercial soilless mix if you are willing to be especially vigilant about fertilizing. Put pot shards or large stones at the bottom of the container for drainage, and then add a mound of soil. Center the rose as you fill up the container with the rest of the soil. Level the soil at the plant's base and water again.

Big containers are heavy to move. What is the solution to this problem?

Buy platform dollies with wheels. Once you have set the containers on the dollies, you can move them about easily.

Can I put newly planted container roses in direct sun?

No. Put them in partial light for a few days, and then move them to a sunny place.

Will indoor roses provide enough flowers for me to cut?

Definitely. If the plants receive ample sun, you will have many flowers for cutting.

If I grow roses indoors, can I also put them outside?

Certainly. Just keep a regular watering and feeding schedule. Be careful not to bring disease-ridden or insect-infested plants back into the house.

Do you cut back larger roses used as houseplants?

Yes. Pruning is necessary, as it is with most roses.

Roses grown under artificial light in homes do well if the right requirements are met. Miniatures are the best choice for artificial light because they do not grow too large. Full-spectrum fluorescent lamps are generally used, although recently incandescent plant "grow lamps" that fit into regular fixtures have proved effective.

GROWING ROSES IN ARTIFICIAL LIGHT

How can artificial light help roses grow?

Today's specially designed grow lamps supply the necessary light rays that plants need in order to grow.

Do I need those elaborate set-ups I see in magazines, with long tubes in fixtures hanging from chains?

No, not at all. A few grow lamps (sold at garden supply stores) will do fine. The fixtures may be wall-mounted; they usually come with instructions.

Which brands of fluorescent lamps are the best?

One brand is as good as another; just make sure that they are grow lamps, and that they meet the needs of your indoor set-up.

How much wattage is necessary to run fluorescent lamps?

Use two 48-inch long, forty-watt tubes.

How can I make my own artificially lit plant stand?

A bookcase-type arrangement, with fluorescent lamps attached to the bottoms of the shelves, works well.

This easily constructed indoor plant stand employs full-spectrum growth lamps.

How close to the lamps should I put the roses? How long should the lamps stay on?

The roses should be three to six inches from the lamps. Lamps should be on for ten to fourteen hours.

I have been told that I should use incandescent lamps along with fluorescents. Is this true?

Both types of lights were used before lamps that have both the attributes of fluorescent (blue) and incandescent (red) light were perfected. Now, standard growth-type lamps are fine.

Won't a standard floor lamp help roses grow?

A standard floor or table lamp (110-watts, for example) will supplement natural light, but by itself will not furnish enough light for roses to bloom. If the roses should bloom, the blooms will be very sparse.

How should I care for roses under lights?

Water the plants more regularly than you would if they were outside, and feed them at least two to three times a month.

Should there be a rest period?

Yes. At some time during winter let the plants dry out a bit, and do not feed them as much. Reduce the amount of time the light is on by three hours daily.

Standards is the technical name for plants grown into treelike shapes. For our purposes, the tree rose, or standard, is a rose bush budded at the upper level of a tall understock stem (the stem and roots of another plant). The charming miniature standards are twelve to sixteen inches tall; tree-sized roses grow to sixty inches. Occasionally you will see weeping rose standards, which are highly dramatic and beautiful. The standards are generally grown in decorative containers and used where a very special accent is needed, say a pair at an entrance, or as vertical accents in a garden room.

Can you grow standards both indoors and out?

They can be grown directly in the ground like any other rose, and they do well in containers, too. They are, however, chiefly outdoor plants.

Will a standard succeed in the home?

Perhaps, but not indefinitely. It is best to grow miniature standards indoors, because they adapt better to home conditions.

Can tree roses be grown in cold climates?

They are difficult to grow in cold climates because they are hard to keep during the winter. In regions where temperatures do not drop below 10° F, they are usually satisfactory.

What kind of rose is most commonly used for a standard?

The hybrid tea is the usual choice, but many of the floribundas, grandifloras, and miniatures will make fine standards.

How should I care for a standard grown in a pot?

Water it as you would a houseplant, and feed weekly with a 10-10-5 plant food through the summer. Prune it back severely to three or four canes in the fall. Use a support for the standard; usually a pole or stake is fine for holding the tree upright. Keep standards in good light, but watch for trunk burn from direct sun.

How do I shape the top?

Occasional trimming and cutting is necessary to keep the head of the rose symmetrical and handsome. Do this before buds set.

ROSE STANDARDS
·

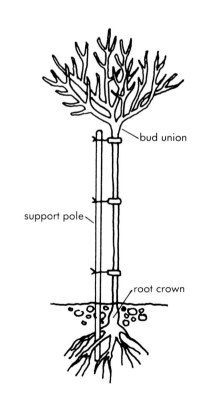

bud union

support pole

root crown

Anatomy of a rose standard.

What are the best varieties to use for standards?

Bewitched is popular as an upright standard, and Chrysler Imperial, another vigorous grower, performs well, too. Queen Elizabeth, a grandiflora, is another common choice.

What is a patio standard?

This is a shorter tree standard, growing to about thirty inches.

How might I use standards in my garden?

They are often planted as vertical accents at intersections of paths. Planted singly or in pairs, they will be focal points among lower growing plants.

Four rose standards define the vertical aspect of this fragrant garden.

1. *Wisteria floribunda 'Longissima Alba'*
2. *Viburnum Juddii*
3. *Prunus tenella 'Fire Hill'*
4. *Syringa Palibiniana*
5. *Cotoneaster apiculatus*
6. *Rosa 'The Fairy'*
7. *Weigela florida 'Springtime'*
8. *Thymus Serpyllum*
9. *Thymus lanuginosus*

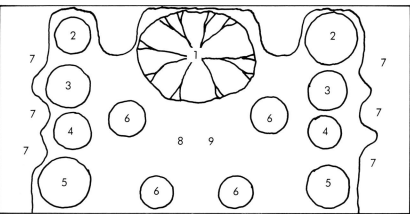

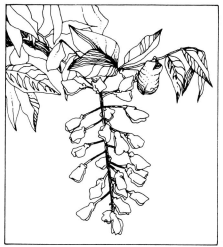

1. Wisteria floribunda 'Longissima Alba'

2. Viburnum Juddii

3. Prunus tenella 'Fire Hill'

4. Syringa Palibiniana

5. Cotoneaster apiculatus

6. Rosa 'The Fairy'

7. Weigela florida 'Springtime'

8. Thymus Serpyllum

9. Thymus lanuginosus

ROSE ARRANGEMENTS

There are many good books about arranging flowers, so this section is only rudimentary, discussing amateur arrangements rather than those of show quality. You don't need to be an expert to make handsome bouquets. Arrangements can be elegant and stately, casual, or dramatic, such as a single rose in a handsome vase. Roses of all one color with some tall background material make an elegant statement. Mixed colors can impart a casual, even festive air.

When should I cut my roses for house decoration?

The best time is in the morning. Using a sharp knife, make a clean cut at a 45-degree angle.

How should I prepare roses for an arrangement?

After cutting them, strip off any leaves or thorns that will be underwater, and put the stems into six or eight inches of water. Let them stand for several hours before arranging them.

How can I remove thorns?

Scrape them away with a small knife, or pull them off with your gloved hands.

These roses are named, appropriately, Sheer Bliss.

Maggie Oster

Derek Fell

Should I cut the bottoms from the stems after they've been in water for a few days?

After two days, cut two inches from the bottoms of the stems at an angle, and put them in fresh water.

How can I anchor roses in the vase so they don't keep moving about?

Use a block of green florist's foam, and don't move the stems about once you've inserted them.

Do you have any special suggestions for arranging roses?

The basic flower arranging rules apply. Do not crowd flowers or use too many colors. Balance the arrangements; that is, include some tall and some medium-height stems. Choose simple containers that don't detract from the roses' beauty.

Are the little packages of chemicals florists give you to keep flowers fresh really necessary?

A cut flower preservative keeps roses fresh longer than plain water does.

My friend says that a copper penny in the water helps keep flowers fresh longer. Is this true?

I don't think so, but there's no harm in trying.

Can you mix roses with other flowers for arrangements?

Certainly, but be choosy because a great many different flowers in a vase can create a cluttered look. Nevertheless, a flower arranger with a judicial and creative eye can mix roses with other flowers to great effect.

Simple, uncrowded arrangements are most effective.

3 *The Major Classes of Roses*

Roses have been around for so long that the many classifications they have been sorted into sometimes confuse the beginning rose gardener. Basically, the field has narrowed down to hybrid teas, floribundas and polyanthas, and grandifloras. The climbers are also popular, as are ramblers, miniature roses, and the old-fashioned roses, which are seeing a renaissance.

The uses for roses are so varied that there are varieties to suit almost any place in the garden. There are even houseplant varieties (the fine miniatures) for inside your home. For the garden there are excellent roses to use as hedges, ground cover, cut flowers, and so on. (See lists in Chapter 1.)

Some gardeners grow hybrid teas for their long blooming season and great variety of colors, others prefer the climbers, and many people favor the old-fashioned roses for their simple beauty. As for cut flowers, we know that nothing expresses our love and appreciation more than a dozen roses given to a special friend or relative. The rose is a highly versatile flower that seems to have universal appeal.

HYBRID TEAS

The hybrid teas are the most widely grown roses worldwide. They come in many different colors, are easy to grow, symmetrically bushy and medium-sized, and can bloom repeatedly. Their ancestry dates back to the nineteenth century, when the European hybrid perpetual roses were crossed with the Chinese tea roses. The late 1800s marked the beginning of a new era in rose cultivation. At first the selection of hybrid teas was some-

◀ Rose Parade (floribunda).

what limited, but by 1900 there were many more varieties, spawned by Soleil d'Or, the first large dark yellow rose that was hardy and bushlike in growth.

Soleil d'Or was not a true hybrid tea, but when it was crossed with one a whole new palette of rose colors—from yellow to orange to copper, bicolors, and so on—resulted. By the 1930s these roses had been crossed a great many times, leading to a robust plant with nicely formed flowers. This robustness owed a great deal to the multitude of crosses that was necessary to create the almost perfect rose. Here, finally, was a long-blooming rose with many uses: for accent, for color, for cutting, for scent, for large beds—quite an achievement over the former weak-stemmed roses that bloomed only a short time.

Why is the hybrid tea so popular?

It has an elegant air about it, grows long stems, and comes in many bright colors. It is the most widely grown rose today.

Are the hybrid teas any more difficult to grow than other roses?

Not really. They require more winter protection in the colder zones, but they are nevertheless easy plants to cultivate.

Is the hybrid tea a prolific bloomer?

Yes, without a doubt. It bears more roses than many other types of roses.

Are there disease-resistant hybrid tea varieties?

Yes: see the others in the section "Roses for Special Places and Purposes" in Chapter 1.

Where would hybrid teas be best in my garden?

In any area where you want a concentration of color and an accent.

Are there many different sizes and heights?

The hybrid teas can be low and spreading or quite tall. Because of the plants' tremendous mixed heritage, there are several different heights and growth habits.

Is the hybrid tea considered the most scented rose?

Many of the teas are fragrant, but I do not think they are any more sweetly scented than other roses.

How long do the hybrid teas flower?

Throughout the growing season, and they bloom profusely.

You mentioned that hybrid teas are popular because of color. What do you mean?

They come in more colors than other roses—the color range is tremendous, including shades of yellow not easily found in floribundas or grandifloras.

Are the flowers longlasting?

Yes, the flowers of some varieties hold color for weeks.

Is it easy to get hybrid teas to bloom?

Even with minimal care your hybrid teas should give you a good harvest of flowers.

What are the flowering times?

They vary according to hardiness zones. In zones 3 through 8 the roses bloom from early summer to frost; in zones 9 and 10 blooming can continue for seven months, starting in the spring. (See map, p. 122.)

What are the hardiness factors of hybrid tea roses?

In zones 6 through 10 most varieties survive without winter protection. In zones 3 through 5 some winter protection is necessary. (See Chapter 5.)

I was told that hybrid teas should always be grown in beds of their own without other shrubs around. Is this true?

Basically, yes. In a mixed planting they do not seem to fare as well, but be willing to experiment.

Ann Reilly

Chrysler Imperial.

Ann Reilly

Swarthmore.

Ann Reilly

Charlotte Armstrong.

Hybrid Tea Roses

NAME	*HEIGHT	COMMENTS
RED		
Allegro	T	Profusion of blooms; mildly fragrant, double flowers.
American Pride	T	Little or no fragrance; large double flowers. Dark green foliage.
Arctic Flame	M	Large double blooms on an extremely hardy plant.
Big Ben	T	Double, fragrant, deep red blooms are large and showy.
Christian Dior	T	All-America Rose Selection 1962. Large well-petaled blooms. Slight fragrance.
Christopher Stone	M	Early blooming, large double flowers; fragrant. Sprawling growth habit.
Chrysler Imperial	T	All-America Rose Selection 1953. Profusely flowering, bushy plant. Rich fragrance.
Crimson Glory	M	Full, velvety flowers; powerful fragrance. Not best in cool climates.
Dave Davis	T	Profusion of large double blooms throughout the season; fragrant.
Dolly Parton	T	Rich-hued orange-red flowers over a long season of bloom. Fragrant. Disease-resistant, robust plant.
Etoile de Hollande	M	Abundant double flowers with a rich, heady fragrance. Compact growth habit.
Firelight	T	Huge double flowers last a long time. Vigorous grower.
Fragrant Cloud	T	Very fragrant, double blooms. Heavy fragrance.
Grand Masterpiece	T	Long cutting stems. Plant is tall and especially vigorous.
Gypsy	T	All-America Rose Selection 1973. Light fragrance. Medium-tall bushes.
Hawaii	M	Very large, double flowers with a sweet, almost fruity fragrance. Robust plant.
Kentucky Derby	T	Pointed to urn-shaped buds.
Mikado	T	Brilliant blend of warm reds; 4- to 5-inch blooms are fully double. Light spicy fragrance.
Mirandy	T	All-America Rose Selection 1945. Outstanding in warm humid regions. Intensely fragrant.
Mr. Lincoln	T	All-America Rose Selection 1965. Satisfactory for all regions. Fragrant. Easy to grow.
Nocturne	M	All-America Rose Selection 1948. Bushy plant. Best in humid regions.
Oklahoma	T	Fragrant. Very deep red. Not at its best in cool, foggy areas.
Olympiad	T	All-America Rose Selection 1984. Light fragrance; long-lasting flowers.

* Height key: S—less than 24 inches, M—24 to 48 inches, T—over 48 inches.

Hybrid Tea Roses
(continued)

NAME	*HEIGHT	COMMENTS
Papa Meilland	T	Fragrant double blooms even in cool, damp weather. Foliage may mildew.
Precious Platinum	T	Foolproof rose. Very heavy bloomer. Husky bush with disease-resistant foliage. Fragrant.
Proud Land	T	Fragrant. Vigorous upright plant.
Red Devil	T	Large, fragrant blooms. Glossy foliage on upright plant.
Red Masterpiece	T	At its best when days are warm and sunny. Rich fragrance.
Red Radiance	T	Double blooms (23 petals). Vigorous and trouble-free.
Rubaiyat	T	Large, fragrant, double blooms. Deep green foliage; hardy plant.
Swarthmore	T	Long-lasting, open flowers. Abundant blooms on upright bush.

PINK

NAME	*HEIGHT	COMMENTS
Bewitched	T	All-America Rose Selection 1967. Fragrant. Vigorous, upright plant.
Century Two	T	Long, full-petaled, fragrant. Upright bushy plant.
Charlotte Armstrong	T	All-America Rose Selection 1941. Large, full flowers; strong, compact plant.
Confidence	T	Large, full flowers; needs warm weather to open properly. Distinct fragrance.
Dainty Bess	T	Five-petaled single blossoms.

* Height key: S—less than 24 inches, M—24 to 48 inches, T—over 48 inches.

Ann Reilly

Electron.

Ann Reilly

Miss All-American Beauty.

Pink Peace.

Hybrid Tea Roses
(continued)

NAME	*HEIGHT	COMMENTS
Duet	M	All-America Rose Selection 1961. Cast-iron constitution; very long-lasting flowers.
Electron	M	All-America Rose Selection 1973. Bushy plant; medium green foliage.
First Love	T	Free blooming; a favorite for cutting.
First Prize	T	All-America Rose Selection 1970. Large flowers. Bushes somewhat susceptible to mildew and blackspot.
Friendship	T	All-America Rose Selection 1979. Always long-budded; good cutting stems.
Futura	T	Moderately fragrant, coral-pink blooms. Vigorous grower; disease resistant.
Helen Traubel	T	All-America Rose Selection 1952. Billowing bushes; rather loose flowers.
Jadis	T	Powerful fragrance. Slender bush; profuse bloomer.
Michèle Meilland	M	Introduced in 1945 but still a favorite. Pale pink, double flowers bloom continuously in singles and clusters. Disease resistant and winter hardy.
Miss All-American Beauty	T	All-America Rose Selection 1968. Very husky plants.
Mon Cheri	M	All-America Rose Selection 1982. Soft pink buds bloom pink-edged, eventually turn to red.
Perfume Delight	T	All-America Rose Selection 1974. Spicy fragrance. Upright, vigorous plants.
Pink Favorite	T	Beautiful shiny green foliage; large, well-formed buds.
Pink Peace	T	Heavy fragrance, blooms throughout growing season. Vigorous upright bushes, prone to rust.
Portrait	T	Rich pink blooms with old-time rose scent. Hardy and disease resistant.
Promise	T	Large and abundant blossoms; foliage is light green.
Royal Highness	T	All-America Rose Selection 1963. Full blooms; upright bushes.
Seashell	M	All-America Rose Selection 1976. Dark green foliage; upright bushes.
South Seas	T	Ruffled, open flowers. Slightly spreading bushes.
Sunset Jubilee	M	Full flowers.
Sweet Surrender	T	All-America Rose Selection 1983. Heady fragrance. Long stems on upright plant.

* Height key: S—less than 24 inches, M—24 to 48 inches, T—over 48 inches.

Hybrid Tea Roses
(continued)

NAME	*HEIGHT	COMMENTS
Tiffany	T	All-America Rose Selection 1955. Intensely fragrant blooms. Upright plant, at its best when not grown in cool, damp regions.
Touch of Class	M	All-America Rose Selection 1986. Heavy-petaled blooms. Large glossy foliage.
Tribute	T	Large open blossoms. Dark glossy foliage.

LAVENDER

Blue Girl	M	Fragrant, profusely blooming, and vigorous.
Blue Nile	T	Fragrant blooms on a bushy plant.
Heirloom	M	Darkest of lavender varieties; fragrant.
Lady X	T	Double flowers on a husky plant.
Paradise	M	All-America Rose Selection 1979. Open blooms; glossy, deep green foliage.
Sterling Silver	M	"Old rose" fragrant blooms. Prune lightly.

ORANGE

Antigua	T	Large shapely blossoms; vigorous plants.
Beauté	T	Large double flowers bloom continuously. Mildly fragrant.
Brandy	T	All-America Rose Selection 1982. Broad-petaled flowers; red-bronze new foliage.
Command Performance	T	All-America Rose Selection 1971. Vigorous, but prone to mildew.

* Height key: S—less than 24 inches, M—24 to 48 inches, T—over 48 inches.

Ann Reilly

Royal Highness.

(Left) Paradise. (Below) Command Performance.

Ann Reilly

Derek Fell

Hybrid Tea Roses
(continued)

NAME	*HEIGHT	COMMENTS
Fragrant Cloud	T	Long buds; husky bush; trouble-free.
Medallion	T	All-America Rose Selection 1973. Large flowers on an upright plant.
Mojave	T	All-America Rose Selection 1954. Vigorous bushes; glossy, medium green leaves.
Pharaoh	M	Deep lilac buds open into large, double, orange flowers with showy yellow stamens. Mildly fragrant. Lovely bronze to bright green foliage.
Seashell	M	All-America Rose Selection 1976. Light orange, fragrant blooms. Mildew resistant.
Smoky	T	Burnt orange to plum blooms with a sweet scent.
Tropicana	T	All-America Rose Selection 1963. Full, cupped, open flowers. Upright, vigorous plant.

WHITE

NAME	*HEIGHT	COMMENTS
Blanche Mallerin	M	Fragrant, double, white blooms. Excellent bud form. A longtime favorite.
Honor	T	All-America Rose Selection 1980. Vigorous plant blooms throughout season.
John F. Kennedy	M	Long buds. Fares best in warm regions.

* Height key: S—less than 24 inches, M—24 to 48 inches, T—over 48 inches.

Fragrant Cloud.

(Below) John F. Kennedy. (Right) Pascali.

Hybrid Tea Roses
(continued)

NAME	*HEIGHT	COMMENTS
Kaiserin Auguste Viktoria	T	Large, double, many-petaled flowers are richly fragrant. Generous first bloom; intermittent after that.
Matterhorn	T	All-America Rose Selection 1966. Profusion of mildly fragrant double blooms on a very tall, upright bush.
Pascali	M	All-America Rose Selection 1969. Flowers in all climates. Upright bush.
Sheer Bliss	M	Sweet fragrance; white blooms with soft pink in center.
Sweet Afton	T	White with blushes of pink; strong fragrance. Spreading and bushy.
White Masterpiece	M	Largest white rose. Resists mildew and blackspot. Protect in winter.
White Knight	M	All-America Rose Selection 1958. Medium-sized double blooms.

YELLOW

Apollo	M	Very large, double blooms. Fragrant.
Arlene Francis	M	Fragrant blooms on spreading bush.
Eclipse	M	Slightly fragrant, primrose yellow blooms. Upright and vigorous grower; needs winter protection.
Golden Masterpiece	M	Largest blooms among roses; color holds well. Upright plant.
Irish Gold	T	Double blooms. Bright green foliage.
King's Ransom	T	All-America Rose Selection 1962. Six-inch flowers. Mildews, but otherwise disease resistant.
Lemon Spice	T	Pale yellow, fragrant blooms. Willowy, vigorous grower. Prolific bloomer. Easy to grow.
Lowell Thomas	M	All-America Rose Selection 1944. Performs well in all regions. Compact bush.
New Day	T	Fragrant blooms. Thorny plant.
Oregold	M	All-America Rose Selection 1975. Bushy. Protect from blackspot, mildew, and winter conditions.
Summer Sunshine	T	Upright and bushy plant.
Sunbright	T	Season-long display of fresh flowers. Upright plant.

MULTICOLOR

Broadway	T	All-America Rose Selection 1986. Strong, upright bush with gold-pink flowers.

* Height key: S—less than 24 inches, M—24 to 48 inches, T—over 48 inches.

Ann Reilly

Irish Gold.

Summer Sunshine.

Ann Reilly

Hybrid Tea Roses
(continued)

Ann Reilly

Double Delight.

NAME	*HEIGHT	COMMENTS
Chicago Peace	T	Magnificent flower form. Pink blooms with yellow at base of petals.
Double Delight	M	All-America Rose Selection 1977. Petals are white with red. Easy-to-grow, spreading bush. Prefers dry climate.
Fascination	M	Apricot, coral, and gold in full flowers. Husky bush.
Flaming Peace	T	Yellow and red flowers. A color sport of Peace.
Forty-Niner	T	All-America Rose Selection 1949. A distinct bicolor; inside is bright Chinese red, outside is yellow.
Garden Party	T	All-America Rose Selection 1960. Ivory with pink edges. Vigorous, but sometimes mildews.
Granada	T	Red and yellow. Strong spicy fragrance. Vigorous, upright, bushy plant.
Headliner	T	Creamy petals edged with cerise. Tall-growing, vigorous, disease resistant.
Kordes' Perfecta	T	Cream-tipped crimson and yellow; heavy fragrance. Upright and vigorous. Burns in direct sun; tends to develop blackspot.
Laura	T	Large salmon and pink flowers in great abundance. Fragrant.
Las Vegas	M	Medium-sized red-orange and yellow flowers.

* Height key: S—less than 24 inches, M—24 to 48 inches, T—over 48 inches.

(Below) Garden Party. (Right) Sutter's Gold.

Ann Reilly

Ann Reilly

Hybrid Tea Roses
(continued)

NAME	*HEIGHT	COMMENTS
Peace	T	All-America Rose Selection 1946. Yellow with pink or red blooms. Strong, spreading bush.
Pristine	T	White with pink blush. Opens well in all weather from urn-shaped buds.
Snowfire	M	Unique rose of deep scarlet with white petals. Compact.
Sutter's Gold	T	All-America Rose Selection 1950. Fragrant yellow-orange blooms. Attractive in cool climates.
Talisman	M	Yellow, orange, and copper buds. Bright green, upright bush.
Voodoo	T	All-America Rose Selection 1986. Yellow, orange, and pink shades in flowers on tall, upright bush.

* Height key: S—less than 24 inches, M—24 to 48 inches, T—over 48 inches.

Derek Fell

Peace.

The Japanese *Rosa multiflora* and varieties of *R. chinensis*, the parents of the polyanthas, appeared at about the same time as the hybrid teas, in the mid-nineteenth century. In the early 1900s the prime characteristic of the polyantha was its large clusters of small flowers, pretty but not elegant.

It was inevitable that the polyanthas, so floriferous, would be crossed with the hybrid teas. The results were a pleasant surprise: better form and larger flowers. These shrubby, large-flowered plants needed a new classification, and so the floribunda class was designated in the 1940s. Since then, floribundas have been crossed so often with the hybrid teas that the resulting rose is now available in almost as many colors as hybrid teas, and the flowers are as large.

If you are a beginner, floribundas are the best roses to start with. They are hardier than other roses and require low maintenance, while providing excellent color. Floribundas will succeed with even rudimentary care: water twice a week, feed every month, and let them grow. Prune the plants lightly, and never worry about them. They seem to resist insects more than other roses.

Are floribundas easier to grow than hybrid teas or grandifloras?

Yes. They are more robust and more free flowering, and they are hardy, too.

How are floribundas best used in the garden?

For a concentration of color—they are frequently used in beds or as border plants.

POLYANTHAS
AND FLORIBUNDAS

Ann Reilly

Bon Bon.

Europeana.

Ann Reilly

Are there certain varieties that are considered tops?

Europeana, Betty Prior, and Iceberg are highly recommended.

Will these roses take city pollution?

To a degree they will, perhaps better than hybrid teas, but they are not pollution-proof.

What is the color range of the floribundas?

Their colors run from white to yellow, coral, pink, red, and a few lavenders.

Is the floribunda a very popular rose?

Yes, but not as frequently grown as the hybrid teas. The floribunda is desirable because it blooms almost continuously in zones 9 and 10, taking only a short winter rest. In zones 3 through 8 it blooms from spring until frost. (See zone map, page 122.)

Is winter protection needed for floribundas?

Yes, they need some protection from freezing temperatures in zones 3 through 7; in zones 7 through 10 you do not need to take any precautions. (See Chapter 5 for information about winter protection.)

Are the floribundas good as cut flowers?

They are, but their flowers generally come in clusters.

What is an ideal way to use floribundas in the garden?

They make superior hedges, or provide color accents massed in beds of their own, and bloom abundantly.

Floribunda Roses

NAME	*HEIGHT	COMMENTS
RED		
Europeana	M	All-America Rose Selection 1968. Fragrant, large clusters of blooms. Low, spreading bush.
Eutin	M	Clusters of slightly fragrant, double blooms. Vigorous grower; disease resistant.
Eye Paint	M	Five-petaled, clustered blooms. Vigorous, bushy plant.
Frensham	M	Tall, vigorous, thorny bush. Excellent as a hedge or background plant.

* Height key: S—less than 24 inches, M—24 to 48 inches, T—over 48 inches.

Floribunda Roses
(continued)

NAME	*HEIGHT	COMMENTS
Garnette	S	Double, rosette-shaped blooms. Foliage susceptible to mildew.
Ginger	S	Slightly fragrant orange-vermilion blooms. Compact and bushy plant.
Interama	M	Brilliant-colored, clustered flowers. Bushy, disease-resistant foliage.
Red Pinocchio	M	Double, carmine-colored blooms. Bushy and branching. Profuse bloomer; good cut flowers.
Sarabande	M	All-America Rose Selection 1960. Especially brilliant flowers. Spreading plants ideal for borders.
Trumpeter	M	Blazing color between orange and red. Disease-resistant foliage.

PINK

NAME	*HEIGHT	COMMENTS
Betty Prior	T	Charm of wild roses. Strong grower with lots of blooms.
Cherish	T	All-America Rose Selection 1980. Robust, vigorous growth. Profusely flowering; blossoms hold color well.
Fashion	M	All-America Rose Selection 1950. Exquisite flowers. Bushy, upright plant.
Gene Boerner	T	All-America Rose Selection 1969. Good repeat blooms of single and clustered flowers. Upright bushes.
Picnic	M	Clusters of slightly fragrant blooms of coral with a yellow base. Can be used for cut flowers.
Rosenelfe	M	Flowers about three inches across. Robust upright plant.
Rose Parade	M	All-America Rose Selection 1975. Spreading, disease-resistant plant.
Sea Pearl	T	Good cut flowers. Vigorous plants.
Simplicity	M	Lavishly flowering shrub, ideal for hedges or mass plantings. Disease-proof foliage.
Vogue	M	All-America Rose Selection 1952. Slender buds; fragrant flowers. Upright bushy plants.

LAVENDER

NAME	*HEIGHT	COMMENTS
Angel Face	M	All-America Rose Selection 1969. Pure lavender flowers grow singly and in clusters. Ruffled, double, fragrant blooms.
Intrigue	S	All-America Rose Selection 1984. Intense fragrance.
Lavender Pinocchio	M	Clusters of double flowers. Vigorous plant.

* Height key: S—less than 24 inches, M—24 to 48 inches, T—over 48 inches.

Ann Reilly

Sarabande.

Cherish.

Derek Fell

Ann Reilly

Angel Face.

Cathedral.

Ann Reilly

Floribunda Roses
(continued)

NAME	*HEIGHT	COMMENTS
ORANGE		
Apricot Nectar	M	All-America Rose Selection 1966. Large flower clusters. Vigorous, winter-hardy bushes.
Bahia	M	All-America Rose Selection 1974. Small clusters of fragrant blooms. Bushy, upright plant.
Cathedral	M	Double, lightly fragrant flowers are good for cutting. Upright and bushy; disease resistant.
Gingersnap	M	Clusters of flowers. Compact plant.
Impatient	M	All-America Rose Selection 1984. Long-lasting three-inch blooms. Dependable and easy to grow.
Margo Koster	S	Small blooms in clusters. Compact bush.
Orangeade	M	Clusters of slightly fragrant orange blooms; good cutting rose.
Spartan	M	Flowers have an old-fashioned look. Vigorous, upright plant.
WHITE		
Evening Star	M	Lightly fragrant blooms. Upright, vigorous grower. Disease resistant.

* Height key: S—less than 24 inches, M—24 to 48 inches, T—over 48 inches.

Floribunda Roses
(continued)

NAME	*HEIGHT	COMMENTS
French Lace	M	All-America Rose Selection 1982. Nearly always in bloom; three- to four-inch, full-petaled blossoms. Disease-resistant, spreading plants.
Iceberg	T	More of a large shrub. Vigorous plant.
Ivory Fashion	M	All-America Rose Selection 1959. Semidouble blooms, longlasting when cut.
Saratoga	T	Fragrant, pure white, disease-resistant blooms. Prolific bloomer.

YELLOW

NAME	*HEIGHT	COMMENTS
Spanish Sun	S	Strong, fragrant blooms. Vigorous grower; compact and bushy. Disease resistant.
Sun Flare	S	All-America Rose Selection 1983. Blooms singly and in three-inch clusters. Active and vigorous, spreading bushy plants.
Sunsprite	M	"Old rose" fragrance. Early blooming roses.

MULTICOLOR

NAME	*HEIGHT	COMMENTS
Bon Bon	M	Showy deep pink and white, moderately fragrant blooms. Spreading plant.
Charisma	M	Lightly fragrant, long-lasting red and yellow flowers. Attractive, upright growth habit.
Circus	M	All-America Rose Selection 1956. Yellow blooms with red at edges. Spreading, glossy foliage.

* Height key: S—less than 24 inches, M—24 to 48 inches, T—over 48 inches.

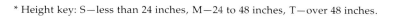

Sun Flare.

Ivory Fashion.

Derek Fell

Redgold.

Floribunda Roses
(continued)

NAME	*HEIGHT	COMMENTS
Circus Parade	M	Orange, buff, and pink blooms on bushy, compact plants.
Matador	M	Sensational as a mass display of scarlet and yellow blooms.
Razzle Dazzle	M	Dazzling red and white bicolor blooms make splendid cut flowers.
Redgold	M	All-America Rose Selection 1971. Buds are yellow, edged with red. Bushy, well-foliaged plant. Plant in sunny spot.
Summer Fashion	M	Ivory and soft yellow with rose-pink margins. Good substance, and sweetly scented.

* Height key: S—less than 24 inches, M—24 to 48 inches, T—over 48 inches.

GRANDIFLORAS

The hybrids of the floribundas and hybrid teas are called grandifloras. This name is appropriate because the flowers of these roses are grand in every sense of the word. The flowers are large, growing on fairly long stems, and almost as profuse as those on the floribundas. The Queen Elizabeth variety is a prime example of a truly magnificent and elegant upright rose.

These fine roses have innumerable uses in the garden landscape. They contribute exquisite accents where a dominant statement is needed because their profuse blooms create a dazzling sphere of color. They can be used for hedges and screening and for background planting. Grandifloras also make exceptionally good cut flowers.

Established as a class in 1954, the grandifloras include many notables, such as Pink Parfait, a tough and handsome rose. The grandifloras often have better than average resistance to disease, and may tolerate quite low temperatures. They require little care (just a bit more than the hybrid teas); primarily some occasional extra pruning.

What is the best-known grandiflora?

Without doubt it is Queen Elizabeth, which was the first of the category. This was a cross between the hybrid tea Charlotte Armstrong and Floradora, a floribunda rose.

Why are grandifloras good selections?

They grow tall and stately, to eight feet or more, and can create a handsome background in gardens. They also produce marvelous cut flowers.

Are grandifloras grown the same way as hybrid teas?

Yes, although they can take somewhat harsher cultural conditions if necessary.

Which would be best in a small garden, grandifloras or hybrid teas?

Use the hybrid teas—they do not grow as tall or as quickly.

Is there as great a color range in grandifloras as in hybrid teas?

No, not really. But these are the newest of all rose classes, established as recently as 1954. More good colors will come along in future years.

Are grandifloras grown much today?

More and more as new varieties come to market. Remember, these roses have been a mere thirty-five years in cultivation, so we will see more of them and use more of them as time goes by.

What attributes make the grandifloras desirable?

The grandifloras combine the finest qualities of their parents as to frequent blooming, hardiness, and abundance of flowers. They are the results of crossing free-flowering floribundas with long-stemmed hybrid teas.

Can you give me the blooming times of grandifloras?

In zones 9 and 10, they bloom continuously for seven months. In zones 3 through 8, flowers are borne from spring until frost. (See map, page 122.)

What is the color range of the grandifloras? You say they are limited in this characteristic.

Their colors range from white to pale yellow, pink, orange, and dark red. There are no lavenders, and only a few grandifloras have bicolor flowers.

What makes grandifloras suitable for cutting?

Their relatively long stems make for fine cut flowers.

I can't tell the difference between grandifloras and hybrid teas. What is it?

I think the main difference is that the flowers of grandifloras bloom in clusters, whereas the flowers of hybrid teas bloom singly.

Derek Fell

Love.

Aquarius.

Derek Fell

Grandiflora Roses

NAME	*HEIGHT	COMMENTS
RED		
Carousel	T	Great for hedges. Vigorous grower.
Comanche	T	All-America Rose Selection 1969. Slightly fragrant, red-orange blooms. Bushy and vigorous grower. Disease resistant.
John S. Armstrong	M	All-America Rose Selection 1962. Many-petaled flowers last for days, cut or on the bush.
Love	M	All-America Rose Selection 1980. Scarlet with white-backed blooms. Vigorous; blooms all season.
Montezuma	T	Vigorous, free branching. Excellent bloomer; superb for cutting.
Olé	M	Long-lasting, double flowers. Bushy grower with hollylike foliage. Very disease resistant. Profuse bloomer.
Scarlet Knight	T	Bloom color holds exceptionally well. New foliage is bronzy green. Very disease resistant. Slight fragrance.
Sonia	T	Long, classic, coral-colored buds unfold slowly. Vigorous, well-branched plant; excellent for cutting.
PINK		
Aquarius	T	Mildly fragrant, medium-sized flowers. Blooms well all season. Mildew resistant.
Camelot	T	Spicy fragrance; pink shadings predominant. Vigorous, upright grower.
Pink Parfait	M	All-America Rose Selection 1961. Perfectly formed buds; good cut flowers.

* Height key: S—less than 24 inches, M—24 to 48 inches, T—over 48 inches.

Grandiflora Roses
(continued)

NAME	*HEIGHT	COMMENTS
Queen Elizabeth	T	Profuse bloomer; excellent cut flower. Nearly disease-proof.

ORANGE

NAME	*HEIGHT	COMMENTS
Arizona	T	All-America Rose Selection 1975. Fragrant blooms on long stems. Resistant to mildew.
Prominent	M	All-America Rose Selection 1977. Longlasting blooms. Thick, dark green foliage.
Shreveport	T	All-America Rose Selection 1982. Medium-sized blooms, mainly on one stem. Mild tea fragrance. Excellent for cutting. Disease resistant.
Sundowner	T	All-America Rose Selection 1979. Profusions of fragrant flowers borne singly and in clusters. Protect from mildew.

WHITE

NAME	*HEIGHT	COMMENTS
Mount Shasta	T	Pure white, moderately fragrant flowers. Upright, vigorous grower. Good cut flowers.
White Lightnin'	T	Ruffled petals with strong citrus fragrance. Bushy plants; mildew-resistant foliage.

YELLOW

NAME	*HEIGHT	COMMENTS
Buccaneer	T	Moderately fragrant blooms; good cut flower. Upright and vigorous.
Gold Medal	T	Rich yellow with red-tinted tips. Vigorous plant; profuse bloomer. Disease resistant.

* Height key: S—less than 24 inches, M—24 to 48 inches, T—over 48 inches.

Ann Reilly

Queen Elizabeth.

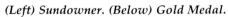

(Left) Sundowner. (Below) Gold Medal.

Jack Barnich

Jack Barnich

CLIMBERS
AND RAMBLERS

I think the many climbing roses are my favorites. They are vigorous, available in many colors, and some can grow to astounding lengths—up to twenty feet. Their drawback is that they must be trained to climb; that is, they have to be tied to or otherwise supported on a trellis or post, or grown against a house wall, or they will become a tangled mess (which can be okay if they are covering an unsightly fence). Climbers are large- or small-flowered; the large flowers of most climbers distinguish them from the small-flowered ramblers.

The ramblers are an older type of climbing rose and have a wonderful old-fashioned look about them. Their long, very flexible canes need some type of support. Ramblers ramble quickly, so they need good pruning to keep them within bounds. Flowering occurs on one-year-old canes. The plants are very hardy and can tolerate temperatures to -20° F.

Climbers and ramblers have me confused. Which is which?

The basic difference is that most climbers have large flowers and ramblers have small flowers. Climbers often bloom twice or more a year; ramblers bloom once a year.

Where are the best garden spots for climbers?

Against a fence or some kind of support where you can train them as they grow. Use twist-ties or twine. Climbers can sometimes grow rampant, so be sure there is plenty of space for them.

Andrew R. Addkison

Ramblers enhace the beauty of this rustic fence.

Where should I grow ramblers?

As with climbers, grow them with support nearby (a trellis, post, or wall) so they will not spread unevenly.

Are there any special soils or planting methods for climbers or ramblers?

No. Plant them in well-drained soil that contains sufficient nutrients. The planting procedure is the same as for other roses. (See Chapter 2.)

Is it absolutely necessary to supply supports for climbing roses?

Yes, climbers (and ramblers as well) naturally sprawl on the ground unless they have suitable trellises or fences to grow against.

Don't the climbers and ramblers have tendrils to grasp poles? They are vines, aren't they?

They are not vines in the true sense, and they do not have tendrils as true vines do.

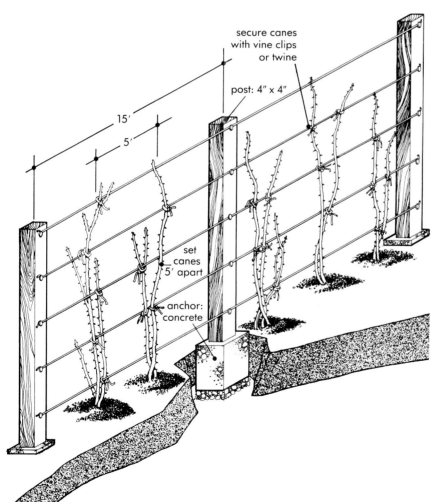

Climbers and ramblers must be supported or they will sprawl on the ground. Here is one way to do it.

Maggie Oster

Climbing First Prize.

What should I use to keep climbers and ramblers tied to supports?

There are standard vine clips sold by garden supply centers, or you can just tie them with twine or cloth strips to a pole or fence. Be sure to wear protective gloves.

Do climbers and ramblers bloom as profusely as hybrid teas?

Yes, they do bloom a lot, but they are slow starters and begin to produce flowers only when their canes are two years or older.

Are there many types of climbers?

Yes. Most of the varieties are large flowered; the ramblers have small flowers. There are climbing versions of hybrid teas, floribundas, and grandifloras.

Could you give me the flowering times for both the climbers and the ramblers?

Climbers generally blossom early in the season, and some follow their first harvest of flowers with another bountiful blossoming later on. Most ramblers, however, blossom once each year—either in late spring or early summer. Only a very few put out a second crop of flowers.

What is the hardiness factor of these roses?

The climbers and most ramblers can usually grow without winter protection as far north as zone 6. (See map, page 122.)

Will these plants survive in very cold winters if I forget to protect them?

Most will—especially some of the ramblers.

What are the color ranges of these roses?

Climbers offer a wide range of colors, with many fine shades of pink and red. Ramblers are limited in color: red, pink, or white. A few are yellow.

What happens if you don't prune ramblers or climbers at the proper times?

No great calamity—they will keep on growing. But pruning is advised to keep them in bounds and growing strongly.

What are some good climbers and ramblers?

For climbers I would use Dortmund, with white-centered red flowers; Handel, with pinked-edged white flowers, and Blossomtime, a fine pink. A good rambler is Chevy Chase, with small red flowers.

Climbing Roses

NAME	*HEIGHT	COMMENTS
RED		
Blaze	T	Clusters of two- to three-inch double flowers. Slight fragrance. Trouble-free.
Climbing Chrysler Imperial	T	Heavy, fragrant blooms. Watch for mildew.
Climbing Etoile de Hollande	T	Blooms rich red in all climates. Vigorous.
Don Juan	T	Pillar climber. Blooms well in most climates.
Dortmund	T	This climber can be used as a ground cover or shrub. Large clusters of flowers.
Joseph's Coat	T	Use as a climber or freestanding shrub. Crimson, mature blooms in clusters.
Kassel	T	Easy climber in mild regions. Scarlet-orange buds, coral-red blooms.
Paul's Scarlet Climber	T	Cluster-flowering. Vigorous; hardier than hybrid tea climbers.
Red Fountain	T	Pillar rose or ten- to twelve-foot climber. Clusters of medium-sized flowers.

* Height key: S—less than 24 inches, M—24 to 48 inches, T—over 48 inches.

Dortmund.

Don Juan.

Maggie Oster

America.

Climbing Roses
(continued)

NAME	*HEIGHT	COMMENTS
Tempo	T	Short for a climber. Double, high-centered individual blooms.
PINK		
Aloha	T	Large, full-petaled flowers.
America	T	All-America Rose Selection 1976. Full blooms, vigorous. Good for growing as a pillar rose.
Climbing Cécile Brunner	T	Easy grower. Small, hybrid tea-style blossoms.
Climbing Charlotte Armstrong	T	Strong-growing, moderate-sized climber.
Climbing Dainty Bess	T	Vigorous climber. Five-petaled blossoms in small clusters.
Climbing Peace	T	A vigorous grower with impressive pink flowers edged with yellow.
Climbing Queen Elizabeth	T	Just as vigorous and prolific as the widely planted bush form.
Climbing Tiffany	T	Hybrid tea available as a climber.
Handel	T	Semidouble pink and cream blossoms in small clusters.
New Dawn	T	Cold-tolerant climbing rose. Flowers come in small clusters.

* Height key: S—less than 24 inches, M—24 to 48 inches, T—over 48 inches.

Aloha.

Maggie Oster

Maggie Oster

Climbing Snowbird.

Climbing Roses
(continued)

NAME	*HEIGHT	COMMENTS
WHITE		
Climbing Snowbird	T	Slender stems. Full, fragrant, flat, open flowers.
White Dawn	T	Medium-sized fragrant blooms. Vigorous and cold-tolerant plant.
YELLOW		
Climbing Talisman	T	Yellow and copper. Vigorous and prolific old favorite. Long cutting stems.
Golden Showers	T	All-America Rose Selection 1957. Profusely flowering, semidouble open blooms. Excellent foliage.
High Noon	T	All-America Rose Selection 1948. Rampant climber.
Piñata	T	Use as small climber. Somewhat shrubby growth.
Royal Gold	T	Natural climber. Blooms come singly or in small clusters.

* Height key: S—less than 24 inches, M—24 to 48 inches, T—over 48 inches.

Golden Showers.

Ann Reilly

MINIATURE ROSES

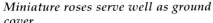

These tiny roses, six to twelve inches high, and with flowers ¾ to 1½ inches across, are miniature replicas of the hybrid tea rose. Recent introductions tend to be a bit larger than former miniatures, so that now the term "macrominiature" is often used to describe the smallest of the minis. Only a few years ago miniature roses were difficult to find; now many mail-order houses specialize in them, and feature dozens of varieties in a wide range of colors. Miniatures offer a world of uses and can be grown both indoors and out.

Why are miniatures suddenly so popular?

Now that they are widely available, people are beginning to recognize their charm.

What are some of their uses?

They can be employed in the landscape just like floribundas, for ground cover, edgings, or borders. Use one variety, one color for a concentration of beauty. They may also be grown indoors.

Miniature roses serve well as ground cover.

Derek Fell

What kind of culture do the miniatures require out-of-doors?

They need the same basic conditions as the other roses: ample water, good drainage, plenty of sun, and moderate feeding.

Do miniatures need pruning?

Yes. At the end of the winter dormant season, cut back the plants to the lowest-growth eyes (dormant buds), or to half their size. This may seem like severe pruning, but in the long run it will ensure a healthier plant.

Will miniatures succeed in the house?

Miniatures make fine indoor plants. Place them near a window but away from hot sunlight, and be sure to feed them regularly. Also, wash the foliage in the sink every week or so to keep insects at bay.

What are their specific indoor requirements?

Daytime temperatures are not too important, but at night the plants like coolness, about 55° to 60° F. Give them high humidity; several plants growing together will naturally ensure this.

What are some of the best miniatures to grow?

My Valentine is a lovely red; Popcorn is a beautiful white; and Baby Darling has pink-apricot flowers. Yellow Doll, Orange Honey, and Dreamglo, a fine red, are other good miniatures.

Miniature Roses

NAME	COMMENTS
RED	
Acey Deucy	Excellent form; bushy.
Chattem Centennial	Double, fragrant flowers. Compact growth habit.
Dreamglo	Tealike buds. Vigorous and longlasting flowers.
Dwarfking	Double, fragrant flowers. Hardy and disease resistant.
Happy Hour	Floriferous, low growing.
High Spirits	Abundant flowers.
Hot Shot	Vigorous; excellent form.
Kathy	Double flowers, floriferous.
My Valentine	Longlasting bloom. Grows well in pots. Disease resistant.
Old Glory	Very large flowers.
Red Imp	Upright, compact bush.
Robin	Compact bush.

Starina.

Bo Peep.

Lavender Jewel.

Miniature Roses
(continued)

NAME	COMMENTS
Samson	Velvety red blooms prefer hot weather. Good cutting flower. Glossy foliage.
Starina	Double flowers with outstanding form; continuous bloom. Good for cut flowers. Star performer.

PINK

NAME	COMMENTS
Antique Rose	Lightly fragrant, double flowers. Strong bloomer.
Bo Peep	Small flowers; compact. A favorite.
Cupcake	Vigorous, free blooming.
Dixie Rose	Double flowers, shapely buds; round form.
Eleanor	Upright, handsome foliage.
Janna	Pretty white edging.
Judy Fischer	Double, good cutting flower. Bushy.
June Time	Bushy, compact plant.
Kathy Robinson	Well-formed flowers with cream-backed petals.
Luvvie	Very small, longlasting flowers.
Peachy	Double, lovely pink flowers.
Pink Porcelain	Vigorous, stellar rose.
Trinket	Small flowers; floriferous.
Willie Winkie	Double flowers. Robust plant.

LAVENDER

NAME	COMMENTS
Angel Darling	Lightly fragrant, ten-petaled blooms. Vigorous, upright bush; winter hardy.
Lavender Jade	Large, full flowers.
Lavender Jewel	Double flowers; blooms a long time. Disease resistant.
Lavender Lace	Fragrant, profusely flowering; good for cut flowers.

WHITE

NAME	COMMENTS
Cinderella	Light pink buds open and fade to white. Compact, bushy plant.
Cottontail	Vigorous. Large flowers.
Green Ice	White with green tinge. Profuse bloomer.
Pacesetter	Beautiful form.
Pixie	Double flowers. Very small, compact bush.
Popcorn	Semidouble flowers; rounded form.
Snow Bride	Fragrant, compact plant
Snowfall	Large flowers.
Starglo	Double blooms. Popular.
White Angel	Double-flowered, fragrant, profuse bloomer.

Miniature Roses
(continued)

NAME	COMMENTS
ORANGE AND YELLOW	
Baby Darling	Double pink to orange or apricot flowers; floriferous.
Bread 'n' Butter	Fragrant. Holds color well.
Ellamae	Blush orange. Good form.
Gold Coin	Compact, shapely yellow flowers.
Holy Toledo	Deep orange with yellow base. Vigorous.
Hula Girl	Large orange flowers. Robust plant.
Jeannie Williams	Small yellow and orange flowers.
Mary Marshall	Double orange flowers with yellow base.
Orange Honey	Excellent shape. Floriferous.
Puppy Love	Double flowers of orange, pink, and yellow; good for cutting.
Rise 'n' Shine	Large yellow flowers. Bushy plant.
Sugar 'n' Spice	Robust grower. Flowers have good substance.
Yellow Doll	Mildly fragrant; profuse bloomer.

Luvvie.

(Left) Green Ice. (Below) Ellamae.

OLD GARDEN ROSES

The old roses, many times called old-fashioned or old-time roses, have gained popularity again in the last few years. Perhaps nostalgia accounts for this, but it is also true that as a rule old roses are tough, robust, tolerant of imperfect growing conditions, and wonderfully fragrant.

The old roses include the classes alba, Bourbon, centifolia, China, damask, gallica, hybrid musk, moss, Noisette, and tea. Each category has different characteristics and something to recommend it to gardeners. Old roses are intriguing plants, and many people collect nothing other.

Years ago old roses were almost impossible to find, but today there are several mail-order houses that specialize in them. (See source list.)

Alba Rose

The alba rose, botanically known as *Rosa alba*, blooms in early spring or in summer. It bears profusions of rather small but pretty white or pink flowers. It is usually a densely growing plant that can reach ten feet, and is very hardy, growing easily in zone 4 (see map, page 122) without winter protection. The plant is nearly impervious to insects or disease.

Maggie Oster

NAME	COMMENTS
Félicité Parmentier	Globular pink flowers flushed with white.
Königin von Dänemark	Pale pink flowers with deep pink centers.
Maiden's Blush	Light pink flowers with a blush.

Maiden's Blush.

Are alba roses hardy enough to grow in New England?

Albas will grow well without winter protection even in zone 4; and since they are also pest- and disease-resistant, they are good choices for northern gardeners.

What is the growth habit of the alba roses?

They are quite tall—up to eight feet—with dense, soft foliage on thorny canes.

Are the albas as flowery as the other old roses?

Yes, they are easy to get to bloom, and they produce many delicate, fragrant flowers, but only once in spring or early summer.

Bourbon Rose

The Bourbon rose, *Rosa borboniana*, is a natural hybrid between the China rose and the autumn damask rose. The Bourbon plant

Derek Fell

La Reine Victoria.

is vigorous and can grow to six feet or higher; it needs a support, such as a trellis or fence. It blooms in midsummer, and again in the fall. The plants are tender and require winter protection in most zones. Their flowers come in a wide range of pink shades.

NAME	COMMENTS
Honorine de Brabant	White flowers striped with pink.
La Reine Victoria	Medium pink flowers, full form.
Louise Odier	Medium pink, double flowers.
Madame Ernst Calvat	Pink flowers on large shrubs or climbers.
Madame Pierre Oger	Pink flowers, rounded blossoms; a sport.

Why is the Bourbon rose so popular?

The Bourbons bloom twice a year, making them very desirable; and they are vigorous growers.

What is the growth habit of the Bourbons?

They are compact shrubs growing to about six feet, and quite floriferous.

Centifolia Rose

When you see huge roses with hundreds of petals you are probably looking at one of the centifolia group, botanically called *Rosa centifolia*. Often called cabbage roses, these plants grow from three to six feet tall, and usually need some kind of support to show them off to best advantage. They bloom once during late spring or early summer. Flower color varies from reddish purple to shades of pink.

NAME	COMMENTS
De Meaux	Pink flowers; a miniature one-inch bloom.
Fantin-Latour	Pale, blush pink flowers; mid-nineteenth century introduction.

Any special tricks to know about the centifolia roses?

They need staking or supports because they produce long, arching canes.

I have been told that centifolia roses have a very strong fragrance. Is this true?

Yes. Their fragrance can be intense.

Did the miniature roses come from centifolias?

It is said that the centifolias are responsible for the first miniature garden roses.

Why is the centifolia rose called the cabbage rose?

Because the flowers have so many petals—as many as one hundred to a flower.

China Rose

China roses, the repeat bloomers of the old rose groups, flower in early summer and then again in the fall. Occasionally certain strong specimens bloom seven months of the year in mild climates. The plants are medium in size with a branching habit; their flowers are borne in large clusters but have little fragrance. Botanically, they are called Rosa *chinensis*.

NAME	COMMENTS
Hermosa	Blush pink, double flowers; nearly thornless canes.
Old Blush	Double pink flowers; abundant bloom.

Maggie Oster

Old Blush.

Are the flowers of China roses large or small?

Medium sized—about two to three inches across, and are mainly available in pink or crimson.

Is it difficult to find China roses?

Because of the renewed interest in the old roses, there are now several mail-order companies that offer them. (See source list.)

Damask Rose

The damask roses, *Rosa damascena*, grow from three to five feet tall (and sometimes to eight feet), are relatively hardy, and quite resistant to disease. They have a rangy growth habit and need proper staking to be at their best. The plants bloom in midsummer, or sometimes in early fall. Damask roses produce tremendous clusters of pink flowers in groups of three or five.

NAME	COMMENTS
Celsiana	Light pink, semidouble flowers are almost white.
Ispahan	Medium pink, double flowers; fragrant.
La Ville de Bruxelles	Rich pink, double flowers; fragrant.
Madame Hardy	White, many-petaled flowers with green eyes.
Madame Zoetmans	Whitish pink flowers.
Marie Louise	Pink flowers.

Celsiana.

What is the growth habit of the damask roses?

Most of them are thorny shrubs with tall, arching canes.

Do damask roses need winter protection?

No, they are quite hardy from zones 4 through 10. (See map, page 122.)

When do damask roses bloom?

They generally bloom once in June or July.

Do all damask roses have a lovely fragrance?

Most all of them do, but it is a moderate scent, rarely strong. Madame Hardy, which is heavily perfumed, is an exception.

Gallica Rose

The gallica, or French, rose goes back centuries; it was grown in many European monasteries and used for herbal remedies. The plants are very hardy, four- to five-foot-tall bushes that will tolerate even the poorest soil and still bloom. The flowers vary

Camaieux.

Derek Fell

Charles de Mills.

from single to double form, mainly in shades of deep red or purple. As easy-to-grow roses they cannot be beaten. *Rosa gallica* is the botanical name.

NAME	COMMENTS
Belle Isis	Pale pink, mildly fragrant flowers with many petals; compact, bushy plant is winter hardy.
Camaieux	Striped, white and red semidouble flowers; upright, bushy plant.
Cardinal de Richelieu	Rose-lavender flowers; large bushy plants.
Charles de Mills	Red-violet, many-petaled flowers.
D'Aguesseau	Red flowers; strong grower.
Duchesse d'Angouleme	Pale pink flowers on a low bush.

I have always liked the gallica, or French, roses. Which are the best, and how do I grow them?

Camaieux and Belle Isis are both fine examples of the old gallica roses. Camaieux is white with red stripes, and Belle Isis is light pink.

Are all gallica roses tall?

No, they grow only to about five feet, but are quite bushy.

When do gallica roses bloom?

Most of these roses bloom only once, in spring or summer.

Are gallicas very hardy?

Extremely so. They do well without winter protection, even in zone 4. (See map, page 122.)

Hybrid Musk Rose

These roses, whose shape and growth habits place them between bushes and climbers, are vigorous plants that bloom in clusters throughout most of the warm months. Some plants can grow to ten feet and require a support (trellis) to look their best. They are less hardy than most of the other old roses, but can be cultivated as far north as zone 5 (see map, page 122) without winter protection.

NAME	COMMENTS
Autumn Delight	Creamy white flowers.
Belinda	Miniature bright pink flowers; grows to six feet.
Erfurt	Multicolor (red with yellow centers).
Kathleen	Blush pink flowers; tall, climbing plant.
Lavender Lassie	Pink flowers; repeat bloomer.
Pax	White flowers.

Maggie Oster

Belinda.

Why are the musk roses so popular?

Their popularity is partly due to the fact that they bloom throughout the growing season. They bear fragrant flowers in large clusters.

What is their habit of growth?

The plants have thick canes and are almost like climbing roses.

Are the musk roses very hardy?

No, not as hardy as other old roses. They must have protection except in zones 5 and below. (See map, page 122.)

Do the musk roses require as much care as other roses?

Usually they do not. They are quite resistant to insects and relatively free of diseases.

The musk roses I have seen all seem to be large plants, almost climbers. Is this true of all musk types?

No, there are smaller varieties that grow to about six feet. Grandmaster and Erfurt are examples.

Moss Rose

These are very large roses that some gardeners call cabbage roses, and they actually are a variant of *Rosa centifolia,* the cabbage rose. The plants have somewhat hairy sepals, which are responsible for the name moss rose. Most varieties have strong canes, heavy with thorns, and grow to about six feet. Like most old roses, they are quite hardy and may be grown in zone 4 (see map, page 122.) without protection.

NAME	COMMENTS
Alfred de Dalmas	Fragrant pink flowers in clusters; winter hardy.
Comtesse de Murinais	White double flowers; needs winter protection.
Deuil de Paul Fontaine	Crimson semidouble flowers bloom singly and in clusters.
Madame Louis Leveque	Pink double flowers; disease resistant and winter hardy.

How did the moss rose get its name?

Moss roses have tiny hairs that coat their sepals and look like moss.

Maggie Oster

Alfred de Dalmas.

Does the moss rose bloom more than once?

No, it is an annual bloomer, usually blooming in spring.

How tall do moss roses grow?

Some are relatively short (to four feet) while others can reach ten feet.

Are moss roses hardy?

Very. They can grow without protection as far north as zone 4.

Noisette Rose

Noisette roses are robust climbers, reaching twenty feet sometimes. This group is a hybrid between the China rose and the musk rose. The flowers are borne in clusters, usually white or pink or yellow, and the bloom time is summer and fall.

NAME	COMMENTS
Blush Noisette	Pale pink double flowers; fragrant; tall, arching canes.
Madame Alfred Carrière	Double, white flowers; fragrant.
Maréchal Niel	Yellow flowers on slender stems; needs winter protection in cold climates.
Rêve d'Or	Yellow-and-salmon flowers.

Are Noisette roses grown much today?

They are having something of a comeback, but because they are tender to temperature extremes they are not widely grown.

What are Noisette roses known for?

They are vigorous climbers and, in zones 8 through 10, generally easy to grow. (See map, page 122.) They bloom for several months at a stretch.

What is the Noisette's flower form?

Usually medium-sized flowers of five to eighty petals, borne in heavy clusters at the ends of the canes.

Shrub Roses

The shrub roses are a versatile group of plants that do not fit clearly into the generally accepted categories. Some are recent or modern rose varieties, while others may be from past centuries. Many gardeners like shrub roses because they have a certain

Ann Reilly

Frühlingsgold.

wildflower quality, they are very hardy, and most bloom prolifically.

NAME	COMMENTS
Frühlingsgold	Red buds create pale yellow flowers with five petals and golden stamens; fragrant; disease free and winter hardy.
Nevada	Large, white, five-petaled flowers bloom in spring and fall; no fragrance; short red canes are almost thornless; disease resistant and winter hardy.
Sea Foam	Creamy white, double flowers bloom in midseason; mild fragrance; trailing canes with small, glossy leaves; disease resistant and winter hardy; sometimes used as ground cover.
Sparrieshoop	Pale pink, strongly fragrant flowers three to four inches across, with five to seven petals; upright, vigorous, bushy plant is disease resistant and winter hardy.

Why aren't the shrub roses included in the other classes?

They don't exactly fit into specific categories such as floribunda or grandiflora, and have varied characteristics, so they are grouped together in the catchall category called shrub roses.

Are shrub roses better than other roses—hybrid teas, for example?

As with all roses, personal selection is most important. If you are the kind of person who likes distinctive plants, these roses may be for you. They are akin to collectors' plants.

What are the advantages of shrub roses?

They are very hardy, and though their flowers are not as large or well formed as those of other types of roses, many have bright red hips in fall. Their flowers have a truly unique, sweet scent.

Do you care for shrub roses the same way as for roses?

The shrub roses do not need as much care as the more popular roses, and will survive if they are forgotten (not watered or fed) for a few weeks.

Tea Rose

The tea rose is an import from China and related to the China rose, but it has larger flowers about three to four inches across. The plants bloom in summer or fall, and are not very winter hardy. Flower colors range from white to pink to yellow.

NAME	COMMENTS
Duchesse de Brabant	Rose flowers, tulip-shaped buds; fragrant; Theodore Roosevelt's favorite rose.
Maman Cochet	Pale pink flowers with yellow bases, painted buds.

Would tea roses be a good choice for my garden?

Most tea roses are thin-stemmed and very susceptible to damage by frost. So unless you are especially fond of the teas' tulip-shaped flower form, other roses would be better choices.

I would like a few old tea roses in my landscape plan. What do you suggest?

I would select Catherine Mermet and Maman Cochet, both relatively resistant to blackspot and mildew. Both have fine, rather large pink flowers.

The species roses share many of the same characteristics as the shrub roses. The true, unaltered species roses are difficult to locate, most having been bred by hybridizers and lost in antiquity. Like the shrub roses, the species roses are very hardy and require little pruning. Most have single flowers. Here is a brief list of the species roses:

NAME	COMMENTS
Rosa eglanteria	The Sweetbriar rose; eight to ten feet tall; single, light to medium pink flowers; fragrant.
R. foetida	Bushy, to four feet tall; semidouble, yellow, fragrant flowers.
R. hugonis	Produces semidouble light yellow flowers; grows to eight feet; prefers poor soil.
R. laevigata	Good climbing shrub rose; white flowers.
R. rugosa	Single carmine-colored flowers from spring to fall; grows in any soil; easy to cultivate.
R. spinosissima	Single pale yellow flowers; low growth habit.
R. wichuraiana	Low growing, spreading plant with single white flowers.

What are the species roses?

These are wild roses, many of which have been crossed to create handsome hybrids classified as shrub roses. *Rosa rugosa* is an old-time favorite.

How do you care for species roses and their hybrids?

Generally, the same as for other shrub roses: not too much food, moderate water, and plenty of sun.

What are some of the hybrids of these species?

Hybrid species roses include F. J. Grootendorst, with crimson-red flowers, Frau Dagmar Hastrup, with a profusion of stunning silvery pink flowers, and Hansa, with large, double, reddish violet flowers.

SPECIES (WILD) ROSES

Ann Reilly

Rosa eglanteria.

Ann Reilly

Rosa foetida.

4 *Propagation and Hybridization*

Many people ask why it is ever necessary to propagate (reproduce) your own roses when plants are usually inexpensive and readily available. The answers are simple: You might want the satisfaction of doing it yourself, or you might want a rose variety no longer available. You might simply be creative. In any case, propagating roses is not difficult and can be fun. There are three ways to do it: from cuttings, from budding, and by cane layering. You can also start roses from seed, but this takes a great deal of time and is simply too much trouble. If you are hybridizing roses to create a new variety, however, seed propagation is worth all the effort and time. There is great satisfaction in creating a new rose or perpetuating some of your favorites that are no longer available.

CUTTINGS

Probably most of us have, at one time or another, taken a cutting from a plant to grow another plant. The process is simple. To obtain a *softwood cutting,* select a stem that is stocky, young, and brittle, and snap it off; spring is the best time. The cutting should be six inches long and have four or five nodes on it. Trim away the lower leaves, retaining a few leaves at the top of the cutting. Dip the bottom end of the cutting in a root hormone preparation (available under various trade names at nurseries), which helps stimulate root development. Insert the cutting to one-half its length into a sterile growing medium (such as vermiculite) in a shallow container with drainage holes. Be sure some of the nodes on the cutting are below the sterile medium line. Keep the

◀ **Rosa wichuraiana**

medium evenly moist and provide adequate humidity (70 percent) and even temperature (78° F). As soon as the cutting shows roots, transplant it into soil in a pot, or in the garden in a somewhat shady place. Move it eventually to a permanent position in the garden.

Some gardeners put cuttings in plastic bags to assure good humidity and even temperature. Similarly, you may root cuttings outdoors by placing them in the open under a glass jar. Be sure to keep the ground moist, and do not let the cuttings receive direct sunlight.

GROWING A ROSE FROM A SOFTWOOD CUTTING

1. Snap a 6-inch stem from a healthy rose bush; trim away the lower leaves.

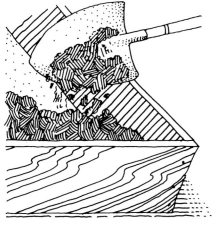

2. Put growing medium in a box.

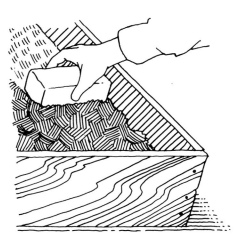

3. Pack down the medium.

4. After dipping the ends of the cuttings in rooting powder, insert the cuttings to half their length in the growing medium.

Is budding the best way to get new roses from your stock?

Most experts agree that the budding method of propagation is superior to other methods, but it does take time, patience, and expertise.

If budding is so difficult, why is it considered the best method of propagation?

Because by budding you are grafting to the rootstock of a more robust plant. The new plant will be a sturdy specimen.

How long should the T-shaped cut be?

No more than one inch long, and it should reach about halfway around the cane.

How do you insert the bud?

The bud is a one-inch slice of bark containing a healthy bud. Open the flaps of the stock and insert the bud (with the bud side out—see illustration). Then press the flaps against the bud.

Where do I get the budding bands you talk about?

These are available at nursery supply stores.

How do I install or wrap a budding band around the cane?

Wind the tape or band above and below the bud, first in one direction, then the other.

How will I know when the bud graft is successful, or if it is successful at all?

In a week or ten days the union will start to swell.

How do I care for new plants made from budding?

The same way you are familiar with—adequate watering and feeding. Begin feeding after the leaves have sprouted and growth is well underway.

CANE LAYERING

Cane layering is a very simple method for getting new roses from old ones. In this process the stems take root while they are still attached to, and nourished by, the mother plant. The cane of the old rose is simply bent low so that part of it can be buried in the ground. Soil layering is the most satisfactory method of layering and works well with any roses that have flexible stems, such as climbers and trailers.

In spring or early summer dig a hole about seven to nine inches deep and about six inches long. Make a shallow cut just below a bud eye in the portion to be buried. Remove the leaves on either side of the cut, moisten the cut, and brush it with rooting hormone. Take two small wood pieces and make a crossed stake. Place this stake below the cut to keep it secure in the ground, and cover it with soil. Set a small stone on top to keep everything in place, and leave the cane buried until the spring. In the spring, while the new plant is still without foliage, remove the soil and cut off the cane near the roots. The new rose is now ready for planting.

PROPAGATING A ROSE BY CANE LAYERING

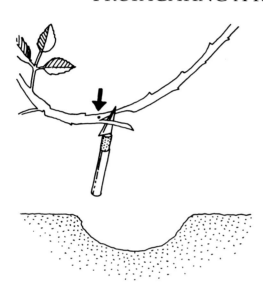

1. Dig a hole 7 to 9 inches deep and 6 inches long; make a shallow cut in a low-growing cane, just below a bud eye.

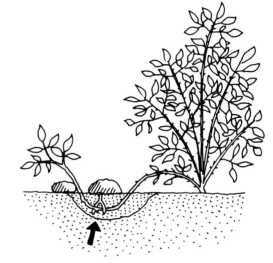

2. Bury the cut portion of the cane, weighting it with a forked stick and a small stone (crossed sticks will work just as well).

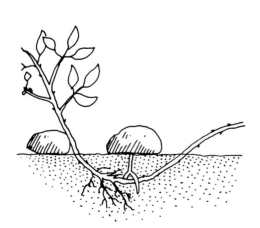

3. Wait for roots to develop.

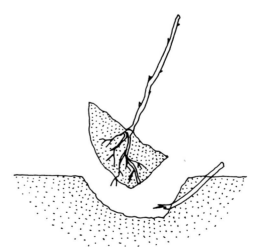

4. In the spring, before the plant leafs out, remove the newly formed root ball and cut it away from the mother plant.

What is cane layering?

It means burying part of a mature cane in a trench. This method is also called soil layering, and is usually done only with roses that have pliable canes.

What are the advantages of cane layering?

It is easy to do and usually successful.

Are there any special rules for cane layering?

Make sure the cane stays buried by weighting it with a stone or two. To further assure that the piece of cane stays underground, place a crossed stake over the buried section.

Does the buried cane draw nourishment from the mother plant? Wouldn't this be harmful to the parent?

The mother plant does provide nourishment, but this doesn't endanger it in any way.

Isn't this layering process for roses the same one used for other shrubs?

Yes, it is the exact same process.

How do I know if roots are developing on the buried section?

If you are anxious, dig up the area and take a peek. It's best to have patience and wait.

What should I do after putting the new plant into the ground?

Simply give it routine care. See that it receives proper nourishment when growth is well underway. (Refer to Chapter 2.)

HYBRIDIZATION

Some rose growers are adventurers who want to create a unique rose that they can call their own. The process of breeding one rose with another is called hybridization. The resultant plant will, it is hoped, excel in some characteristic: bigger flowers, better form, heightened disease resistance, and so on. In most regions you can hybridize with the first crop of bloom in spring. Cross-pollination of roses is the method of transferring pollen from the anthers (male organs) of a flower to the pistil (female organs) of another flower from a different plant. The process involves some work, but it is not especially complex.

How long does it take to make a new rose?

Figure on at least a couple of years, or two springs, to get a mature-looking plant.

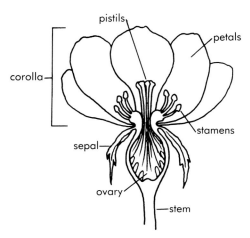

Anatomy of a flower.

What is the first step in hybridization?

Choose blossoms from two varieties of plants when petals are just beginning to unfold. Roses are bisexual, which means that each flower is both male and female. You can use a flower from one plant as a male and a flower from the other as a female, or vice versa—it doesn't matter which. Put the "male" bud stem in water. Remove all petals from the "female" bud. With tweezers, pull off the female's male stamens so self-pollination does not occur.

After I choose the parents of the new rose plant, how should I proceed?

Put a small paper bag over the stripped buds to protect them from insects, then remove the bag after a day or so to see if the pistils are somewhat sticky. Next, rub the male's stamens over the female's flower pistils.

How will I know if the pollination is successful?

Inspect the female's flower pistil to see if any orange or yellow grains of pollen are on top. If there are no pollen grains, start again.

HYBRIDIZING A ROSE

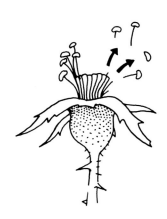

1. *Select an open bloom and remove its petals and stamens to prevent self-pollination.*

2. *Cover the stripped flower with a bag.*

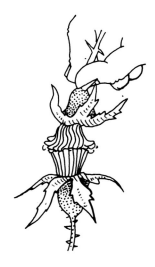

3. *Make the cross, when the stigmas have become sticky, by cutting a flower with pollen-laden stamens, discarding its petals, and rubbing its stamens on the stigmas of the prepared bloom.*

If pollination is successful, what next?

Place a small paper bag over the female flower again. Take it off after one week. If the flower's base has swollen, the job has been done. It will take several months for the hip (seed pod) to mature, at which time remove it for later planting. The seeds are inside the hip.

How do I start the seeds?

Start seeds (be sure they are plump and not hollow) one inch apart in a sterile planting mix, in a flat four-inch box. Put their parental names on the box and place the box in the refrigerator crisper at about 40° F. Keep the box there for about six weeks, and then move it to a bright window with a temperature of 55°-60° F.

When should I remove new plants from the flat or box?

In about a month, once new growth shows and leaves are sprouting. When the seedlings have three leaves, transplant them into their own container. By the following spring the young plants should have leaves and their first flowers. Take the most promising seedlings and graft them onto the rootstock of hardier varieties, or simply plant them in open ground.

Can't I just take rose hips from my mature plants in the garden and follow the same process?

These may be self-pollinated plants rather than cross-pollinated. To ensure an altogether new rose, you must pollinate one rose variety with another and then grow hybrid plants from the seed.

Are there any special precautions for this seed-starting hybridization process?

Yes. Damping-off is frequently a problem. This is caused by a fungus that rots young seedlings at the soil line. Be sure to use a sterilized soil or potting medium and clean containers.

5 *Preventive Care for Roses*

Roses attract their fair share of insects, but the bugs can be eradicated quickly; pest control is no longer the problem it once was. If diseases strike, there are remedies. With good observation and the proper selection of preventives, you can grow roses easily without their being overcome by insects or disease. You may not have to resort to chemical warfare at all, because old-fashioned remedies such as hosing off insects will often solve the problem. Of course, a plant grown in good conditions will be healthy and better able to ward off pests. Insects are more likely to attack weak plants.

ROSE CULTURE

The best way to maintain healthy plants is to provide good growing conditions and to catch trouble before it starts. A few insects caught in their first days can be eradicated easily, but in a week or ten days they may become a major force, because insects breed quickly—very quickly. Mealybugs, for example, are capable of producing thousands of young in a few days. So catching trouble in time means keen observation. Keep your roses well groomed by picking off dead leaves and faded flowers which promote disease.

Plants that are failing (indicated by discolored leaves or prematurely dropped buds) are not necessarily suffering from an attack of insects or disease. Poor culture can also harm plants. The plants may need new soil to facilitate good water drainage, or a different method of watering. If your roses exhibit any of the

◀ *White Dawn.*

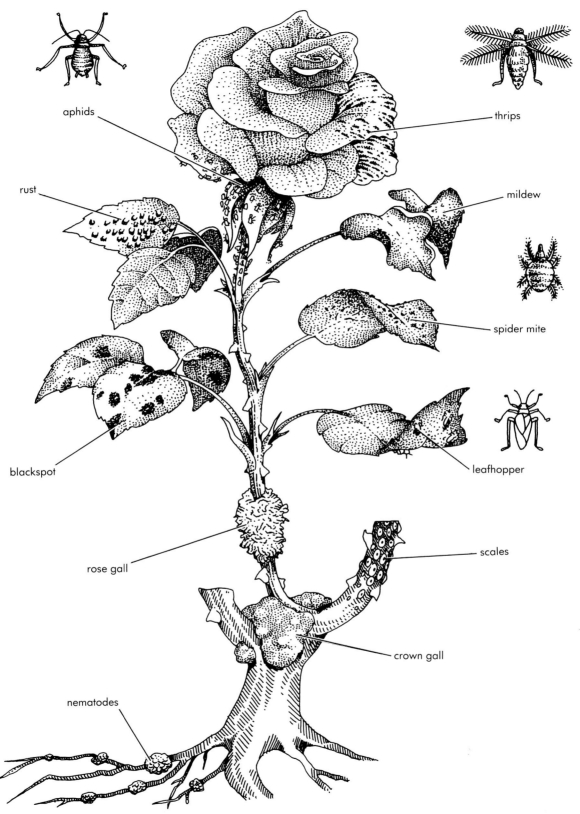

aphids

thrips

rust

mildew

spider mite

blackspot

leafhopper

rose gall

scales

crown gall

nematodes

Pests and diseases.

102

following symptoms, look for the cause of the problem before you reach for chemicals or take any other symptom-treating measures:

Symptoms of Poor Rose Culture

SYMPTOMS	CAUSES
Leaves are not fresh green. Weak growth.	Too little sun, heat too high.
Brown or yellow leaves.	Soil is either too dry or too wet. Not enough or too much humidity.
Slow growth.	Soil may not be draining properly, or plants may be in their natural rest state.
Leaves drop.	Rapidly changing or extremely fluctuating temperatures.
Yellow or whitish rings on foliage.	Watering with icy water.
Buds drop.	Extreme temperature fluctuation. Humidity too low.
Dry crumbling leaves.	Humidity too low.

INSECTS

If you have purchased healthy plants and provided optimum cultural conditions, but the plants are still not growing properly, it is time to look for insects as the cause of the trouble. Some of the culprits, such as scale and mealybugs, can be seen. Other pests, such as red spider mites, are almost invisible to the naked eye.

Many insects lay eggs, but some (aphids are a good example) produce living young. These are called nymphs, and they have different coloring from the adults. They may be wingless or winged, depending upon the species. All plant-sucking insects, and some chewing ones, go through a gradual transformation as they mature. Some insects upon maturation look completely different from their immature-stage appearance.

Chewing insects are fast feeders and can rip and tear edges of leaves, make holes in foliage, and even skeletonize leaves. These insects range from various types of caterpillars to many different kinds of beetles. Sap-sucking insects attack a plant from the stem to the growing tip of the roots. They suck out plant juices and can cause leaves to become stippled, yellow, brown, or wilted. Aphids, leafhoppers, and thrips are in this category.

Rose gall, which usually affects species roses rather than hybrids, appears as swellings on roots or stems. The gall, or swelling, is caused by wasplike insects that get into the canes and lay eggs. Insecticides do not really control rose gall; the best procedure is to prune away any infected stems before the eggs hatch into larvae.

Nematodes signal their presence with pale green foliage and an overall stunted look to the plant. If you examine the roots of an infested plant you will see swelling, and knotty areas with tiny white eggs inside. You can use all-purpose soil fumigants to eradicate these pests; some nematocides are also available. Check with the Agricultural Experimental Station in your area for aid in diagnosis and control. (State Agricultural Stations are in the phone book.)

Botanical insecticides—and many commercial rose care products contain these substances—are not persistent and harmful to man or land. Pyrethrum and rotenone are the two most popular repellents. Check the labels of conventional sprays to be sure that these botanicals are not being used in combination with persistent poisons such as Dieldrin or Chlordane, for example.

Pyrethrum is derived from a species of chrysanthemum with a daisylike flower. The pulverized flowers are toxic to insects. Pyrethrum kills aphids, whiteflies, leafhoppers, and thrips on contact.

Rotenone comes from the derris plant, a woody climber with purple and white flowers. Its root is ground into an effective powder that wards off aphids, spider mites, chinch bugs, and harlequin bugs.

Rotenone or pyrethrum are available in liquid form or in granules. Carefully follow the directions on the packages when you apply these preventives to your roses.

Just how much pest control do roses need?

Not much. Years ago, controlling various insects was a problem, but not so today. There are many effective control methods.

Is there any way to determine when pests might attack?

Most insects appear when the weather turns warm, about 70° F, because this is when conditions are favorable for them.

How will I know if insects are attacking my plants?

Leaves may be eaten at the edges; they may be yellow or brown; or they may simply fall off. Stems may wilt.

Are all such problems with roses caused by insects or disease?

Many times poor growing conditions will bring on the same symptoms as insects or disease will. If all conditions are right and your plants still suffer, look for insects.

Can you tell me exactly which insects to look for?

Aphids—small oval-bodied yellow, black, green, or brown critters—are easy to see. They resemble plant lice and suck juices from leaves. Look for them on stems and at leaf axils. Beetles and caterpillars may attack leaves, and you can see their work immediately. The almost microscopic rose midge does its damage in the larval stage. It deposits eggs in new growth, and the larvae hatch and eat the tender new growth. Borers attack new growth; sudden wilting or drooping signals their existence in your garden.

Can you elaborate on mites?

These almost-invisible pests suck cell sap from leaves, causing them to yellow or turn orange. A good hosing down helps control them.

What can I do about these insects?

Most are easy to eradicate. Homemade concoctions control many insects, and there are chemicals to use if absolutely necessary. See the chart of old-fashioned controls below.

Common Rose Pests

SYMPTOMS	CAUSE	OLD-FASHIONED CONTROL
Undersized leaves, spindly growth.	Mealybugs—white cottony clusters in stems, leaf axils.	Try washing the plant with soapy water and rinse thoroughly with clear water, or dip a cotton swab in alcohol and apply directly to insects.
Silvery streaks on leaves, or deformed foliage.	Almost invisible yellow or black-brown sucking insects called thrips.	Wash plants with soapy water, and rinse with clear water, or sprinkle paprika or pepper on the soil.
Sooty mold on leaves or stems, stunted growth; sticky or shiny leaves.	Oval-shaped insects called aphids. These common green, black, red, or pink pests appear on new growth.	Apply cotton swabs dipped in alcohol directly to aphids, or give them a strong blast of water from a hose.
Leaves mottled or crumbly; shiny streaks on leaves.	Almost invisible spider mites.	Spray plant vigorously with soapy water and rinse.
Leaves turn pale, mottled.	Tiny, oval, hard-shelled brown or black insects called scale.	Try picking off the insects, or scrub the leaves with a homemade nicotine solution (use old cigarettes steeped in water for two days). Or use nicotine sulfate, available at nursery supply centers.
Leaves stippled or very faded.	Small flying insects called whiteflies.	Use a strong spray of water, or sprinkle pepper on the soil.
Holes in leaves, or edges of leaves eaten.	Slugs and snails.	Use beer or half-cut potatoes as bait. Destroy captives.
Leaves eaten, growth spindly.	Caterpillars, beetles; easily seen.	Handpicking works but is hardly pleasant. Laundry soap and water solution thwarts the culprits.
Tender new growth eaten, plant stunted.	Rose midge; difficult to see. Tiny yellow flies lay eggs, maggots hatch and eat tissue.	Remove and destroy affected areas.
Plant shoots wilt; holes in canes.	Borers, which eat into canes and lay eggs.	Cut away affected canes; treat exposed ends with pruning paint.

How can I minimize the possibility of disease attacking my roses?

Plant your roses where there is good air circulation. This will minimize foliage diseases to a great extent.

Do I have to use chemicals to combat pests and disease?

No. Use the old-fashioned remedies, such as those indicated in the chart on page 105. Organic gardening is possible, even for roses.

If I do use chemicals to control insects, how should I apply them?

Use either a spray or a dust. Both work well, though dusting must be done on a windless day to prevent drifting chemicals. Dusting is easier because no mixing is involved—just put the powder in the applicator and start to work. Spraying requires more work but can be most effective. You will need some type of sprayer, and the concentrated chemical must be mixed with water.

What are the advantages of spraying?

Spraying gets to all parts of the plant: leaf axils, undersides of leaves, and so on. It does a better job of thoroughly protecting the plant than dusting.

When is the best time to apply sprays or dusts?

Early morning or early evening.

Do you have any suggestions for properly dusting roses?

Do not apply a heavy coating of dust—a light sprinkling is sufficient. Dust when the air is still.

Are there any specific directions for spraying with insecticides?

Spray the morning after you have thoroughly watered, and never spray in the heat of the day. Do not drench the plant; light spraying is best. Spray both the tops and undersides of leaves, and all canes and stems. Be sure the plant is dry by evening. Also, wear protective clothing, and read all labels carefully.

Can you explain the differences among the various plant protection processes?

Nontoxic control, which is done with old-fashioned methods rather than chemicals, is best because it's safest. Contact poisons kill insects or disease by direct contact. Systemics are toxic chemicals that the plant absorbs, making its sap poisonous to insects who suck plant juices. Systemic protection lasts a few months at most.

Of all the insects that attack roses, which are the worst?

Aphids and mites. These bugs can be tough to get rid of unless you are very diligent and spray regularly.

Are the manufacturers' directions for the use of chemicals as important as they make themselves out to be?

Absolutely. Follow directions on packages to the letter. Keep all chemicals on a very high shelf or in a locked medicine cabinet, far away from children.

Will these chemicals make my pets ill?

Certain ones will, others will not. Again, read *all* the print on the packages, bottles, or cans.

DISEASES

Plant diseases occasionally strike roses. Most are not easy to get rid of, so be alert to the various symptoms of diseases so you can prevent trouble before it happens. No one wants a costly rose ruined by botrytis blight or mildew, and a little knowledge put into action can often save a stricken plant. Ailments that afflict plants manifest themselves in various ways: spots or mildew on the leaves, rotting at the crown, and so on. Because many plant diseases cause similar external symptoms, it is important to identify the specific disease so you can use the appropriate remedies.

Unfavorable growing conditions such as too little or too much humidity, extreme heat or cold, or insect infestation can contrib-

Ann Reilly

This new foliage is covered with mildew.

ute to plant disease, which is caused, in general, by bacteria and fungi. Bacteria enter the plant through minute wounds and small openings, and then multiply and start to break down plant tissue. Animals, insects, soil, and dust carry bacteria that can attack a plant. So do people. If you have touched a diseased plant, you can carry the disease to healthy plants. Tools such as scissors can carry disease, so sterilize tools with a flame or with alcohol after using them. Rotting leaves, spots on foliage, and wilts come from diseases caused by bacteria.

Like bacteria, fungi enter a plant through a wound or a natural opening. Their spores are carried by wind, water, insects, people, and equipment. Fungi multiply very rapidly in damp, shady conditions because moisture is conducive to their reproduction. They cause rusts, mildew, blights, and some forms of leaf spot. Good air circulation goes a long way in keeping fungi and bacterial infections from striking plants.

Here are the principal plant diseases and what to do when they infect a plant:

I have heard so much about rose diseases. How bad are they?

Not as bad as you may have heard. Blackspot, powdery mildew, and rust are the big three to watch for, but all can be controlled. (See chart.)

Is there any way of preventing mildew on roses?

This is virtually impossible because the disease is spread by the wind. Warm days and cool nights also bring on mildew. You will have to battle mildew with the proper controls. (See chart.)

Is virus in roses always fatal to the plant?

No, but it is a very difficult disease to arrest. Fortunately, many rose varieties are now virus-free.

Principal Rose Diseases

SYMPTOMS	CAUSE	CONTROL
Gray or watery-green leaves.	Bacterial blight	Remove infected plant parts and apply charcoal dust to the wounded areas.
Coated white leaves.	Powdery mildew	Wash with water. Dust affected areas with charcoal dust; systemic Benomyl control.
Gray mold on leaves, flowers.	Botrytis blight	Discard infected plant.
Leaves, flowers, and stalks spotted with concentric rings.	Virus	Destroy (burn) infected plants because there is no real cure.
Leaves fall; black spots on foliage.	Blackspot	Good garden sanitation. Do not crowd roses. Systemic control: Funginex. Or try Benomyl.
Rusty-orange areas on undersides of leaves. Powdery masses of large spores. Defoliation.	Rust	Keep garden area clean. Remove old leaves. Systemic control: Funginex.

Ann Reilly

This foliage has rose blackspot disease.

You don't mention crown gall. Doesn't this attack roses?

This soil-borne bacterial disease can be a problem. Remove and burn infected parts (or entire infected plants), and replace the soil that the plants were growing in (or treat it with a fumigant). The best way to avoid crown gall is to buy healthy plants, and to practice good garden sanitation. Avoid spreading the disease in your garden by sterilizing shears and other tools that have been in contact with infected plants or soil.

Can you tell me something more about blackspot?

Blackspot is a fungus disease easily spread in the garden. The disease overwinters in debris on the ground, so good sanitation goes a long way in remedying this problem.

I have heard that faded flowers should always be picked and disposed of. Why is this?

This practice discourages fungus diseases, including botrytis blight.

Is Benomyl a very poisonous substance? It is often recommended for rose diseases.

Any chemical may be toxic; there is no guarantee that any one in particular is safe.

If I must use chemicals to combat disease, which can I depend on to work the best?

I think the systemics are best. They're easy to use and do protect the plant from disease.

WINTER PROTECTION

Winter protection for roses is necessary in most parts of the country. You can use simple or complex protection, depending on whether or not you are a perfectionist. Simple procedures will usually do the job. Winter injury results from rapid and frequent temperature changes, as well as low temperatures. Moisture in the canes contracts during freezing, causing cell walls to break.

Winter winds can dry out canes, and frozen soil prevents roots from taking up moisture. Thus in spring you find blackened or shriveled canes. As a rule, winter protection is necessary for most roses when temperatures drop to 15° F, though some roses can take lower temperatures.

In the United States and Canada the hardiness zone map, prepared by the Agricultural Research Service of the United States Department of Agriculture, is used as a guide for what you can and cannot grow in your particular geographical region (see page 122). There are, however, exceptions to each of the numbered zones. These *microclimates* are areas in your garden where certain influences alter the general temperatures: a fence facing south will accumulate heat; a hill sloping away from the house will be cooler. Warm air rises and cool air sinks, so gardens in hilly terrain have several microclimates. Houses can serve as windbreaks, and the heat that radiates from their walls can warm the surrounding air. Large bodies of water also affect the minimum temperature within a zone. They temper the overall climate of the adjoining areas and can raise an area's classification one full zone from inland regions.

What is a good, easy way to protect my roses in the winter?

Mound up eight inches of soil against the bushes. Do this after frost, but before the ground freezes.

Would some type of covering work, too?

Styrofoam cones do the job, but first tie the plants' canes together. Hold the cones in place by placing a brick on top of them.

What about the burlap coverings that I use for my other plants?

This method works well. Make sure to tie the burlap around the canes. It's also important to mulch around the roots with soil or leaves.

Should I protect all my roses the same way for winter?

Yes, except for your climbers, which should be covered and wrapped with burlap, or laid down on the ground and covered with soil. Tree roses (standards) also need to be laid down and covered with soil.

WINTER PROTECTION METHODS

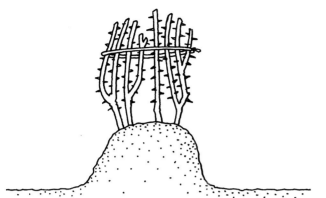

Mound soil at least 8 inches over each bush.

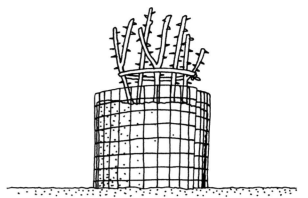

Cylinder of wire mesh holds mounded soil in place around canes.

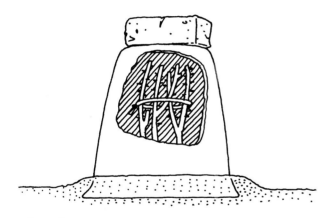

Styrofoam rose cones.

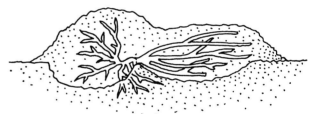

Trench protection.

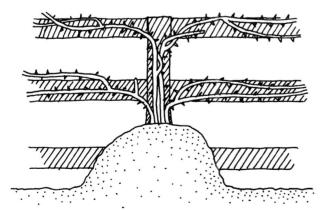

Protect climbing roses with soil mound.

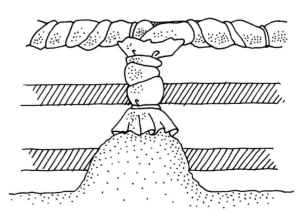

Insulate canes with burlap.

When should I remove the winter protection?

After the frost is over—usually in early spring, depending on where you live. Resist the temptation to remove winter protection early. Remember that the weather is fickle, and cold days may return after a few warm ones.

If some canes are damaged from winter burn, should I discard the plant?

Just cut away the damaged parts and dust the cuts with charcoal. Continue to care for the plants as usual.

Do all roses need winter protection?

Some are hardier than others; check with local rose growers in your area for recommendations.

How should I protect the roses I am growing in tubs on my patio?

You can overwinter them in an unheated garage. Roses in large containers (at least fourteen inches in all directions) can be left outside in many areas of the country. Ask around to find out what other rose growers in your area are doing.

MULCHING

Mulching is a procedure that can eliminate weeding, prevent a hard crust from forming on the soil, reduce the amount of water roses need, and reduce the likelihood of disease by providing a barrier between infected material on the ground and the developing leaves on the plant. The disadvantages of mulches are that they are not always attractive, they take time to apply, and some of them add nothing to the soil. Many nonmulchers argue that if you space roses correctly (so that the leaves of one bush almost touch the other) the ground will be shaded and cool; this way you will reduce water evaporation and discourage weeds.

What are the best mulches?

An organic mulch, such as old tree leaves, adds nutrients to the soil. Grass clippings and hay are also excellent. Depending on where you live, you may be able to find buckwheat hulls, cocoa shells, ground corn cobs, wood chips, pine needles, or rice hulls.

What are some of the inorganic mulches?

Some of the most popular are black plastic film, polyester fabric (both sold at nurseries), and gravel.

What about the bagged pieces of bark I see at nurseries?

Bark is a fine mulching material. It is attractive and longlasting.

Ann Reilly

Mulching reduces weeding, watering, and cultivating requirements and helps prevent the spread of disease.

How do I apply a mulch?

Apply loose mulch around the base of the plant in a circle. Hold black plastic film and polyester fabric in place with stones.

When should I apply a mulch?

In the spring, after the ground has warmed up a little.

Appendix

The American Rose Center, operated by the American Rose Society (ARS), contains more than 118 acres of woodland just outside of Shreveport, Louisiana. The center is a vast test and demonstration garden.

The *American Rose Magazine* and the *American Rose Annual* are valuable and exciting publications to the rose enthusiast. Subscriptions to both are included with membership in the ARS. Supported by thousands of members nationwide, the American Rose Society is one of the largest plant societies. Each year it holds the National Rose Convention, at which prizes and awards are given for achievements in work with roses. To join the American Rose Society, write to American Rose Society, P.O. Box 30,000, Shreveport, LA 71130.

There are many national rose societies and thousands of local rose societies around the world. England's Royal National Rose Society, established in 1876, was the first. All national rose societies are united by the World Federation of Rose Societies. Following are four of the largest rose societies:

The Canadian Rose Society
20 Portico Drive
Scarborough, Ontario
Canada MIG 3R3

Royal National Rose Society
Chiswell Green Lane
St. Albans
Hertfordshire, England

Japan Rose Society
4-12-6 Todoroki
Setagaya-ku
Tokyo, Japan

ROSE ORGANIZATIONS

National Rose Society of Australia
340 Union Road
Dalwyn
Victoria 3103, Australia

SOME AARS DISPLAY GARDENS

Please check with the local chamber of commerce before visiting any of these locations—changes of address are made occasionally.

Alabama

Battleship Memorial Park, Battleship Memorial Pkwy., Mobile

David A. Hemphill Park, Springdale Plaza, Airport Blvd., Mobile

Arizona

Valley Garden Center Municipal Rose Garden, 1809 North 15th Avenue, Phoenix

California

Arcadia County Rose Garden, 405 S. Santa Anita Avenue, Arcadia

Berkeley Municipal Rose Garden, Euclid Avenue at Bay View Place, Berkeley

Fresno Municipal Rose Garden, Roeding Park, Fresno

Descanso Gardens, 1418 Descanso Drive, La Canada

Los Angeles City Garden, Exposition Park, 701 State Park Dr., Los Angeles

Morcom Amphitheater of Roses, Head of Jean St., one block off Grand Ave., Oakland

Fairmount Park, 2225 Market St., Riverside

Capitol Park, 15th and Capitol Ave., Sacramento

San Jose Municipal Rose Garden, Dana and Naglee, San Jose

Huntington Botanical Gardens, 1151 Oxford Rd., San Marino

A.C. Postel Memorial Rose Garden, Mission Historial Park, 400 E. Plaza Rubio, Santa Barbara

Rose Hills Memorial Park Pageant of Roses Garden, 3900 S. Workman Mill Rd., Whittier

Colorado

Denver Botanic Gardens, City Park, 18th and Colorado Boulevard, Denver

Longmont Lions Club Memorial Rose Garden, 700 Longs Peak, Longmont

Connecticut

Elizabeth Park Rose Garden, 160 Walbridge Rd., West Hartford

District of Columbia

Shoreham Hotel Rose Garden, Between G and H, 20th and 21st Sts.

Florida

Walt Disney World, Lake Buena Vista

Georgia

Greater Atlanta Garden, Piedmont Park, The Prado, Atlanta

Callaway Gardens, Rt. 27, Pine Mountain

Hawaii

University of Hawaii Maui Agricultural Research Center, Kula

Idaho

Municipal Rose Garden, Julia Davis Park, Boise

Illinois

Gardener's Memorial Garden, 1707 St. John's Avenue, Highland Park

Glen Oak Botanical Garden, 2218 N. Prospect Ave., Peoria

Indiana

Lakeside Park Rose Garden, 1500 Lake Avenue, Fort Wayne

Iowa

Iowa State University Horticultural Gardens, Sixth and Haber, Ames

Vander Veer Park Municipal Rose Garden, 216 W. Central Park Ave., Davenport

Greenwood Park Rose Garden, 45th through 49th Sts., Des Moines

Weed Park Memorial Rose Garden, Muscatine

Kansas

Kansas State University Rose Garden, Manhattan

Kentucky

Kentucky Memorial Garden, Kentucky Exposition Center, Louisville

Louisiana

Louisiana State University Rose Variety Test Garden, South Campus Dr., Baton Rouge

Municipal Rose Gardens, Bolivar Boulevard, Bienville Plaza, New Orleans

American Rose Center, 8877 Jefferson-Paige Rd., Shreveport

Maine

Deering Oaks Park Rose Circle, 227 Park Ave., Portland

Maryland

Brookside Botanical Gardens, 1500 Glenallen Ave., Wheaton

Massachusetts

James P. Kelleher Garden, Park Dr., Boston

Stanley Park of Westfield, 400 Western Ave., Westfield

Michigan

Michigan State University Horticultural Gardens, E. Circle Dr., East Lansing

Frances Park Memorial Garden, 2600 Moores River Dr., Lansing

Minnesota

Lyndale Park Municipal Rose Garden, Roseway Rd. and E. Lake Harriet Pkwy., Minneapolis

Mississippi

Hattiesburg Area Garden, Campus of University of Southern Mississippi, Hattiesburg

Missouri

Cape Girardeau Rose Display Garden, Capaha Park, Broadway and Perry Ave., Cape Girardeau

Laura Conyers Smith Municipal Rose Garden, Jacob L. Loose Memorial Park, 52nd and Pennsylvania, Kansas City

Missouri Botanic Garden, 4344 Shaw Blvd., St. Louis

Montana

Missoula Memorial Rose Garden, 700 Block of Brooks St., Missoula

Nebraska

Lincoln Municipal Rose Garden, Antelope Park, 2740 A St., Lincoln

Memorial Park Garden, 57th and Underwood Ave., Omaha

Nevada

Reno Municipal Rose Garden, 2055 Idlewild Dr., Reno

New Hampshire

Fuller Gardens, 10 Willow Ave., North Hampton

New Jersey

Brookdale Park Garden, Bloomfield

Jack D. Lissemore Garden, Davis Johnson Park, 137 Eagle St., Tenafly

New Mexico

Prospect Park Garden, 8205 Apache Ave. N.E., Albuquerque

New York

Edwin deTurk Bechtel Memorial Garden, New York Botanical Garden, Bronx

Cranford Memorial Garden, Brooklyn Botanic Gardens, 1000 Washington Ave., Brooklyn

Joan Fuzak Memorial Garden, Erie Basin Marina, Erie St., Buffalo

Sonnenberg Gardens, 151 Charlotte St., Canandaigua

Queens Botanical Garden, 43–50 Main St., Flushing

United Nations Garden, New York

Old Westbury Gardens, 71 Old Westbury Rd., Old Westbury

Central Park Garden, Wright Ave. and Central Pkwy., Schenectady

Dr. E.M. Mills Memorial Garden, Thorndon Park, Ostrom Ave. and University Pl., Syracuse

North Carolina

Raleigh Municipal Rose Garden, 301 Pogue St., Raleigh

Ohio

Columbus Park of Roses, High St. at Acton Rd., Columbus

Ohio State University Rose Garden, Columbus

Oklahoma

J.E. Conrad Municipal Garden, Honor Heights Park, 641 Park Dr., Muskogee

Municipal Rose Garden, Will Rogers Park, 3500 N.W. 36th Street, Oklahoma City

Tulsa Municipal Rose Garden, Woodward Park, 21st and Peoria Ave., Tulsa

Oregon

Corvallis Community Rose Garden, Avery Park, Corvallis

George E. Owen Park Municipal Rose Garden, 301 N. Jefferson St., Eugene

International Rose Test Garden, 400 S.W. Kingston Ave., Portland

Pennsylvania

Malcom W. Gross Memorial Garden, 2700 Parkway Blvd., Allentown

Hershey Memorial Gardens, 621 Park Ave., Hershey

Longwood Gardens, Kennett Square

Marion Rivinus Garden, Morris Arboretum, 9414 Meadowbrook Ave., Philadelphia

Robert Pyle Memorial Garden, West Grove

South Carolina

Edisto Rose Garden, Edisto Memorial Gardens, Calhoun Dr., Orangeburg

South Dakota

Memorial Park Garden, 444 Mt. Rushmore Rd., Rapid City

Tennessee

Municipal Rose Garden, Warner Park, 1254 E. Third St., Chattanooga

Memphis Municipal Rose Garden, Audubon Park, Memphis

Texas

Samuell-Grand Municipal Garden, 6200 E. Grand Blvd., Dallas

Municipal Garden, 1702 Copia St., El Paso

Fort Worth Botanic Garden, 3220 Botanic Garden Dr., Forth Worth

Houston Municipal Garden, 1500 Hermann Dr., Houston

Brown Center Gardens of Lamar University, 4205 Park Ave., Orange

Tyler Municipal Rose Garden, Tyler

Victoria Garden, Riverside Park, 480 McCright Dr., Victoria

Utah

Salt Lake City Municipal Rose Garden, Sugar House Park, 1602 E. 2100 St., Salt Lake City

Virginia

American Horticultural Society, River Farm, 7931 E. Boulevard Dr., Alexandria

Bon Air Memorial Garden, Bon Air Park, Wilson Blvd. and Lexington St., Arlington

Bicentennial Rose Garden, Norfolk Botanical Gardens, Airport Rd., Norfolk

Washington

Aberdeen Municipal Rose Garden, Samuel Benn Park, Aberdeen

Fairhaven Park Rose Garden, Bellingham

Woodland Park Garden, 5500 Phinney Ave. N., Seattle

Rose Hill, Manito Park, Four W. 21st. Ave., Spokane

West Virginia

Ritter Park Rose Garden, McCoy Rd., Huntington

Wisconsin

Alfred L. Boerner Botanical Gardens, Whitnall Park, 5879 S. 92nd Street, Hales Corners

Olbrich Gardens, 3330 Atwood Ave., Madison

MAIL-ORDER SUPPLIERS

There are several mail-order suppliers of roses; some issue catalogs free, others have a minimal charge that is usually refundable upon the purchase of plants. The following companies are those I have dealt with and know—it is not a complete list, and the inclusion of a company here is not meant to be an endorsement.

The Conrad Pyle Co.   *fine selection*
372 Rose Hill Rd.
West Grove, PA 19390

Heritage Rose Gardens
16831 Mitchell Creek Dr.
Fort Bragg, CA 95437

old roses

Jackson & Perkins
Medford, OR 97501
(503) 776-2121

large selection

Kelly Brothers Nursery
650 Maple St.
Dansville, NY 14437
(716) 335-2211

shrub and species roses

Mini-Roses
Box 4255 Station A
Dallas, TX 75208

miniatures

Nor'East Miniature Roses, Inc.
58 Hammond St.
Rowley, MA 01969
(617) 948-7964

*miniatures; large
selection*

Pixie Treasures
4121 Prospect Ave.
Yorba Linda, CA 92686
(714) 993-6780

miniatures

Rosehill Farm
Gregg Neck Rd., Box 406
Galena, MD 21635
(301) 648-5538

Roses of Yesterday and Today
(formerly Tillotson's Roses)
802 Brown Valley Rd.
Watsonville, CA 95076
(408) 724-3537

old roses

Sequoia Nursery, Moore
Miniature Roses
2519 E. Noble Ave.
Visalia, CA 93277
(209) 732-0190

miniature roses

Stocking Rose Nursery
785 N. Capitol Ave.
San Jose, CA 95133
(408) 258-3606

*nice selection of modern
roses, including a few
novelty cultivars*

Thomasville Nursery
P.O. Box 7
1842 Smith Ave.
Thomasville, GA 31792

*some old roses, and
many modern varieties*

Tiny Petals Miniature Roses
489 Minot Ave.
Chula Vista, CA 92010
(619) 422-0385

miniatures

Wayside Gardens
Hodges, SC 29695-0001

complete garden catalog

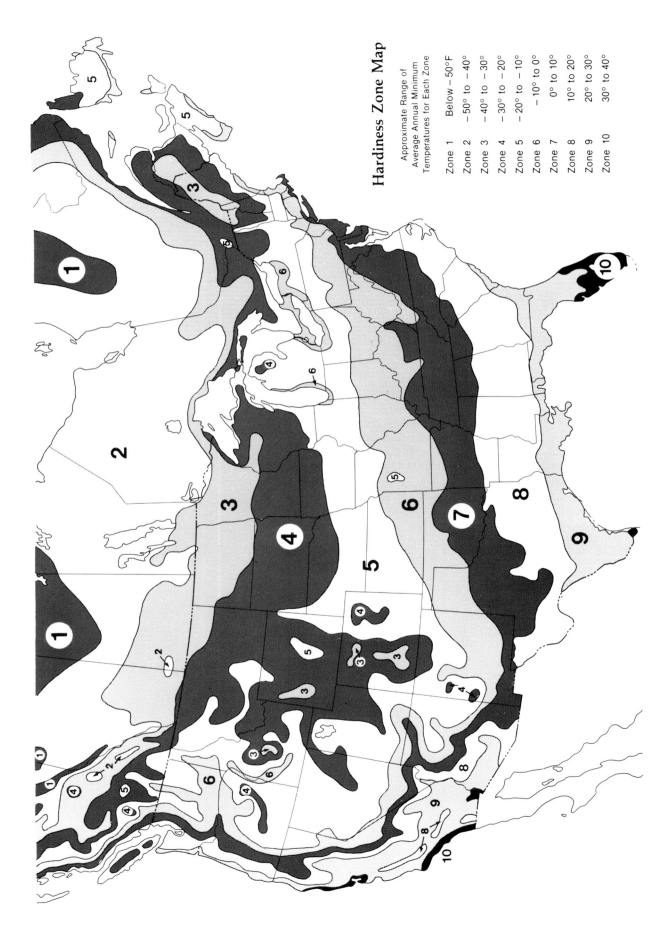

Hardiness Zone Map

Approximate Range of
Average Annual Minimum
Temperatures for Each Zone

Zone 1   Below −50°F
Zone 2   −50° to −40°
Zone 3   −40° to −30°
Zone 4   −30° to −20°
Zone 5   −20° to −10°
Zone 6   −10° to 0°
Zone 7   0° to 10°
Zone 8   10° to 20°
Zone 9   20° to 30°
Zone 10   30° to 40°

Glossary

ANTHER. The pollen-bearing tip of the stamen.

BARE ROOT. A plant sold without soil around its roots.

BUD. An unopened flower. It also can mean the growth or eye where leaves join stems. "To bud" means to take the growth eye and start a plant from it by grafting.

BUD UNION. This is the part of the plant where topgrowth joins the understock one to three inches above the roots. It is a knob that grows larger each year.

CANES. The principal stems of the rose plant. They form the plant's structure.

CLASSIFICATION. The system whereby roses are put into easily recognizable categories such as shrub roses, old garden roses, etc.

CLOCHE. A cone-shaped covering, often of plastic, fiberglass, or glass, to protect roses from frost or winter conditions.

CULTIVAR. A hybridized rose registered with the American Rose Society.

DOUBLE FLOWERS. Flowers with twenty-four to fifty petals.

HARDWOOD CUTTING. A mature five- to six-inch cane.

HIP. The seed pod that forms after a flower's petals fall. Many turn brilliant colors.

JOINTS. Bulges on canes where new growth begins.

MACRO-MINIATURE. A term given to a rose that is smaller than a miniature.

MULCH. Any material that, arranged to cover the soil around a plant, prevents water evaporation, keeps the ground cool, and prevents weed growth. Mulches may be biodegradable or synthetic and thus fairly permanent.

NODES. See joints.

OVARY. The enlarged, seed-containing base of the pistil.

PATIO ROSE. Same as a standard but shorter in height, to about thirty-six inches. Recently introduced.

PISTIL. The female reproductory organ of a flower. Consists of an ovary, a style, and a stigma.

PLANT PATENT. Some new rose introductions are patented. The patent holder and the rose's originator receive a percentage from the sale of each plant for seventeen years.

RAISED BEDS. Planting beds in which the soil has been mounded to a level higher than the surrounding soil. Raised beds are often used in intensively planted gardens.

SEMIDOUBLE FLOWERS. Flowers with six to eighteen petals.

SOFTWOOD CUTTING. A tip cutting from a rose—a five- to six-inch section of stem used for propagation.

SPECIES ROSE. A wild rose unchanged from its natural form.

SPORT. A chance, naturally occuring change in habit or flower color in an established variety; sometimes called a mutation.

STAMEN. The male reproductive organ of a flower. Consists of an anther and a filament.

STANDARD. A rose bush budded high on an understock stem, also called a tree rose.

STIGMA. The tip of the pistil. Grains of pollen are trapped by its sticky surface during pollination.

STYLE. The stigma-bearing stalk of the pistil, extending from the ovary.

SUCKER. Any growth emanating from below the bud union. This growth should be removed.

UNDERSTOCK. A rose that furnished the root system for budded plants.

VARIETIES. Different versions of a species; sometimes used interchangeably with the word *cultivar*.

Bibliography

All About Roses, Editors, Staff of Ortho Books, 1983.

Anyone Can Grow Roses, Cynthia Westcott, D. Van Nostrand, 1952.

The Complete Book of Roses, Gerd Krussmann, Timber Press, 1985.

The Concise Handbook of Roses, Eigil Kiaer, E.P. Dutton and Co., 1966.

Growing Roses, Michael Gibson, Timber Press, 1984.

The Rockwells' Complete Book of Roses, Doubleday and Co., Inc., 1957.

Roses, James Underwood Crockett, Time Life Books, 1971.

Roses, Roger Phillips and Martyn Rix, Random House, 1988 (originally published in London by Pan Books).

Roses: How to Grow, Editors of Sunset Books, Sunset-Lane, 1980.

Index